L. Moon

A journey of faith and sacrifice
Retracing the steps of Lottie Moon

A journey of faith and sacrifice
Retracing the steps of Lottie Moon

Written by Jerry Rankin  Photography by Don Rutledge

Foreword by Dellanna O'Brien

New Hope

Birmingham, Alabama

New Hope
P.O.Box 12065
Birmingham, AL 35202-2065

©1996 by New Hope
All rights reserved. First printing 1996
Printed in Mexico

Dewey Decimal Classification: 266.009
Subject Headings: MISSIONS, FOREIGN
                              MOON, CHARLOTTE DIGGS (LOTTIE) 1840-1912
                              MISSIONS—CHINA—PICTORIAL WORKS
                              FOREIGN MISSION BOARD, SBC—HISTORY
                              MISSIONARIES, FOREIGN

Scripture taken from the NEW AMERICAN STANDARD BIBLE ®,
    ©Copyright The Lockman Foundation 1960, 1962, 1963, 1968, 1971,
    1972, 1973, 1975, 1977. Used by permission.

Cover and book design by Dan Beatty

ISBN 1-56309-188-7

N964152*0596*4M 1

Digital pre-press done by Repro 1, Inc., Richmond, Virginia
Printed by RR Donelley & Sons Company, Reynosa Division

edicated to the more than 12,000 Southern Baptist missionaries who have been appointed by the Foreign Mission Board and served our Lord Jesus Christ around the world in the spirit of faith and sacrifice of Lottie Moon.

Southern Baptist missionary Lottie Moon entered China through the port at Yantai—then called Chefoo—in 1873.

CONTENTS

f through a time warp, Charlotte Digges Moon could return to her land of birth, she would be astonished that her name is a household word in the homes of Southern Baptists in our day. Although we have no official saints in our denomination, Lottie Moon would, no doubt, be first on the list if such a practice were instated.

Sent out in 1873 as Southern Baptists' second fully appointed woman missionary, Lottie found her place of service in the Shantung Province of China. Through the years, she overcame obstacles few of us could imagine in order to share the good news of Christ. She identified so completely with the Chinese people, that she gave even her life in responding to their needs.

A selfless, unassuming lady, she never sought acclaim. Perhaps that is the reason members of the new Executive Committee of the Woman's Mission Societies, forerunner to Woman's Missionary Union, were first challenged to do the extraordinary in 1888.

The money Lottie requested of these ladies was not for herself, rather it was to provide for two other women to join her and other Southern Baptist missionaries in China. Annie Armstrong, first elected executive director, used the enormous sum of $72.82 to promote this first offering for foreign missions, with a goal of $2,000. When the offering was counted, these early mission supporters had gathered enough to send three women to Lottie's aid.

For the first time Southern Baptist women demonstrated the difference they could make together in the support of missionaries through prayer and giving.

Today when Southern Baptists give their special foreign missions offering, the symbol of its purpose is Lottie Moon. While her life epitomizes the sacrificial lifestyle, she also represents thousands of other missionaries, less well known perhaps, but equally faithful to the Great Commission.

As you read this book, you will be inspired by rediscovering the achievements of the past. You will be informed of the status of the church today and challenged in the opportunities for sharing Christ throughout the world in our future. Join Jerry Rankin and his wife, Bobbye, on a pictorial journey through Lottie Moon's China—truly a journey of faith and sacrifice.

—*Dellanna O'Brien*

Winter sun peers through a tree in Albemarle County, Virginia, where Lottie Moon grew up. From Albemarle, she would trade one-half of the globe for the other, traveling and teaching in at least six cities of Shantung Province, North China. Everywhere she went, the missions pioneer left a bit of light—stretching across miles, minds, and hearts.

'I wonder how many of us really believe that it is more blessed to give than to receive. A woman who accepts that statement of our Lord Jesus Christ as a fact, and not as "impracticable idealism," will make giving a principle of her life.'

—Lottie Moon, September 15, 1887

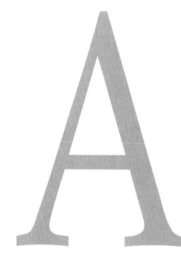

As long as I can recall, I have known the name of Lottie Moon. I was reared in a church characterized by a strong missions emphasis, and the Lottie Moon Christmas Offering for Foreign Missions was—as far back as I can remember—a high point on our church calendar. In our part of the country, the Lottie Moon theme echoed throughout every Southern Baptist church during the month of December. Long before I was born, long before I started attending First Baptist Church of Clinton, Mississippi, the Lottie Moon Christmas Offering had become a cornerstone of the church's Christmas season.

First Baptist stood across the street from Mississippi College, where foreign mission service was a major focus among the students. God had earlier called people from our church to serve Him overseas as missionaries, and people talked about those missionaries with admiration. Others, including college students, frequently walked forward during worship service altar calls in response to the challenge to "surrender" to missionary service. Furloughing missionaries returned to share the intrigue and adventure of confronting distant cultures with the Christian message.

In that context, the name Lottie Moon seemed synonymous with foreign missions and giving to foreign missions. In our community, giving to Lottie Moon was as much a part of the Christmas season as trimming the tree and other holiday festivities. I recall collecting coins in special little tin-can banks, and participating in the Sunday morning parade down the church aisle to place them on the altar for Lottie Moon.

"Who was this Lottie Moon?" some asked even back then. Many still ask that question as they are challenged to give to missions in her honor. As a child, all I knew was that she was a missionary to China. Each mention of her name would bring to mind an elderly couple who faithfully occupied the same pew on the right side of our church every Sunday. I knew them as Mr. and Mrs. Hendon Harris, retired missionaries to China. But in my childish mind I couldn't make the distinction between this wrinkled pious lady with her gray hair tied in a bun who had been a missionary in China, and Lottie Moon, the missionary to China for whom

The building which housed the church in Huanghsien, the first founded by Lottie Moon, in the P'ingtu area, is gone. But Lottie Moon's legacy lingers not only in this monument to Li Show Ting, an evangelist she converted and discipled, but also in Li's grandnephew (left) and this young boy who is part of the Christian congregation still meeting in Huanghsien. Such a long-standing ministry only could have survived, and thrived, through the caliber of obedience to God exhibited by Lottie Moon— and by others who have followed her example.

the offering was named. I would look at Mrs. Harris in awe, and wonder, "Is this Lottie Moon?"

As a child in Sunbeams and later Royal Ambassadors, I was captivated by the story of Lottie Moon, told to us along with accounts of contemporary missionaries as if she were still alive. And in a sense she is; her calling and sacrificial commitment continue to inspire hundreds of Southern Baptist missionaries who still follow in her steps.

When I think of Lottie Moon, another person who comes to mind is Elizabeth Hale. "Aunt Elizabeth," as her mission- ary colleagues fondly called her, was like Lottie; she also came from Virginia and served in China for many years. When the doors closed to China in the early 1950s, she trans- ferred to Malaysia to continue a ministry among the Chinese there. I met her years after her retirement to "Bethel Hill," as her home near Alor Star on the Malay Peninsula was called. She had refused to return to the United States and, into her late seventies, continued her ministry overseas. She always wore thong sandals and pajama-like Chinese clothes, and kept her long, plaited hair pinned on her head. That demon- strated not just her identification with the Chinese in appear- ance and lifestyle, but her total dedication and selflessness.

As I grew older, still another person came to personify Lottie Moon to me: Bertha Smith. From her retirement as a missionary until her death at age 99, "Miss Bertha" carried out a unique ministry of calling Christians to holiness and Spirit-filled lives. In her earlier missionary years, she had been a part of the Shantung Revival in 1928-32, a phenomenal outpouring of God's Spirit in China that brought believers and unbelievers alike to their knees in repentance for their sins. With unusual boldness and candor, she confronted churches and individuals with a call to that kind of repentance—much as Lottie must have done when she called Southern Baptists to task for their lack of commitment to missions. Like Lottie, "Miss Bertha" was a short woman who towered over most others because she exuded a deep, no-nonsense spirituality.

For more than fifty years—as I moved from childhood to maturity, as I responded to God's call, as I served churches as a pastor, and as I served for twenty-three years as a missionary in Southeast Asia—Lottie Moon was a beloved tradition to me. She represented a legacy with which any missionary can identify. Sadly, many Southern Baptists today don't know the person behind the legend. They see the Lottie Moon Christmas Offering as nothing more than just another denominational program designed to raise money during the Christmas season.

After becoming president of the Foreign Mission Board, I felt compelled to dig deeper and discover what made the legend of Lottie Moon so captivating to successive genera-

tions of Southern Baptists. What has made her appeal powerful enough to motivate our denomination to give a total of more than $1.5 billion[1] to foreign missions over the years in her memory?

In 1995, as we celebrated the sesquicentennial of the founding of the Foreign Mission Board and the Southern Baptist Convention, I decided to pursue my interest further. It seemed appropriate because we are nearing the end of the century and preparing to enter a new millennium. I knew it was important to review the past to gain insight for the future. Looking back to Lottie Moon's history through such works as Catherine Allen's *The New Lottie Moon Story* and Una Lawrence Robert's *Lottie Moon*, I gained a deeper respect for all those who had gone out before us with vision and determination. I gratefully acknowledge the influence of these and other historical works about Lottie Moon on this book. I also want to acknowledge with deep appreciation the assistance David Button, the Foreign Mission Board's Vice President for Public Relations and Development, provided me in researching and writing this book.

As the year 2000 approaches, we Southern Baptists confront unprecedented opportunities to proclaim the gospel to the whole world. Old barriers to the gospel have fallen in many countries. Record numbers of missionaries are being appointed. We have entered an era of growth and potential for much greater growth. We stand on the threshold of actually being able to carry out the Great Commission to preach the gospel to every person on earth.

This era did not just happen. Those whom God has been calling out for the past 150 years of foreign mission service—including many who have given their lives in distant and hostile lands—have laid a magnificent foundation for our era. Because of their obedience to the call, their suffering, and their sacrifice, Southern Baptists today serve in more than 130 countries and report record baptisms and church growth.

The roll call of these early missionaries and their experiences would parallel those heroes of the faith listed in the 11th chapter of Hebrews. Lottie Moon was not alone, but she certainly epitomized those who, like Abraham, "when he was called, obeyed . . . and he went out, not knowing where he was going. By faith he lived as an alien . . . in a foreign land . . . All these died in faith . . . having confessed that they were strangers and exiles on the earth . . . men of whom the world was not worthy. . . ." (Heb. 11:8-9, 13, 38).

I was delighted to discover that the Foreign Mission Board building in Richmond, Virginia, is not far from "Lottie Moon country." She grew up in Albemarle County near Thomas Jefferson's home, Monticello, little more than an hour's drive from Richmond. I felt a visit to these historic landmarks, and retracing her steps in China, would bring Lottie out of the history books and enhance the relevance of her life to what God is doing today in China and throughout the world.

Just as He did for the young Lottie Moon, God continues to reach down and touch young people—even rebellious ones like Lottie once was—to call them to submission to Him. Just as He did in 1873 to Lottie, God continues to touch schoolteachers, pastors, medical workers, businessmen, and people in all sorts of professions. He continues to give them a burden for the lost—compelling them to leave the security and comforts of home to face the unknown on a distant mission field.

China was the primary Southern Baptist mission field in Lottie's day.[2] Today God is opening all sorts of new doors and calling those who will respond to challenging places such as Mongolia, Uzbekistan, and Azerbaijan, as well as the traditional mission fields of Asia, Africa, Europe, and Latin America. The sacrifice and hardship Lottie faced is not a relic of the nineteenth century; it is as contemporary as today in many of the countries God has recently opened.

A century ago it took weeks or months to travel the world on sailing ships, trains, and horse carts. Today, jets deliver the contemporary missionary to places of service in a matter of hours. Communication technology links missionaries overseas with their support base at home for instantaneous reports and appeals for prayer and financial needs. Missions methods have changed, living conditions have improved dramatically in many parts of the world, and travel is easier. But the world still wanders in spiritual darkness—lost and groping for God. The Father still calls us to share the world's only hope of salvation: Jesus Christ. The message is the same, the need is undiminished, and the responsibility to proclaim the gospel is unchanged from the day Lottie Moon first boarded a ship bound for China, where she spent almost forty years and literally gave her life.

When Lottie left for China, world population barely topped 1 billion. Today, China alone has more people than that, and the world's population is approaching 6 billion. Our mission researchers tell us that as many as 1.7 billion still have not heard the gospel of Jesus.[3] Yet God's kingdom is being extended throughout the world. Believers are planting churches among some people groups who are hearing the gospel for the first time. There is every reason to believe the prophecy of Jesus will be fulfilled that "this gospel of the kingdom shall be preached in the whole world for a witness to all the nations, and then the end shall come" (Matt. 24:14).

But the calling is still urgent, and the needs as overwhelming as ever. Lottie Moon modeled the obedience and faithfulness God expects of us today as we respond to the mandate of our Lord: "Go therefore and make disciples of all the nations" (Matt. 28:19).

A Chinese proverb speaks to the heart of missionaries who have heard and responded to the call of God, regardless of the obstacles and the pitfalls that blocked their path: A journey of a thousand miles must begin with a single step.[4]

That first step can be considerably different today from what it was in the nineteenth century. Nevertheless, it still must be taken. In my quest to understand Lottie Moon more fully, I decided to retrace her steps. Even though I had served as a missionary in Indonesia and a missions leader in southeast Asia for a number of years, I had never been to China. The Chinese culture and societies in Singapore, Malaysia, Hong Kong, and Taiwan are quite familiar to me, but I felt a sense of excitement at the thought of visiting China for the first time.

We flew to Yantai in northern China and immersed ourselves for days in the places where Lottie lived, taught, and worked. Through her schools and itinerant rural ministry, she introduced the people in the cities then known as Tengchow, P'ingtu, Huanghsien, and other nearby villages to her Savior. As we walked the streets she walked and saw living conditions that seemed to have changed little since her day, we could easily imagine that diminutive missionary courageously mingling with the people. Many of the buildings of her era were gone, but the churches were there. Believers had persevered in their faith because of the sound doctrine and example of sacrifice Lottie and her missionary colleagues gave to the Chinese people.

This legacy to the power of the gospel continues to encourage me as I seek to guide the Foreign Mission Board in reaching people who have never heard of the saving power of Jesus Christ. But the most emotional and gripping impression of the journey was seeing the millions of people living in those cities and villages who are still lost without Christ.

It occurred to me that Lottie must have perceived what the proverb implies: The journey never ends. Her journey did not end when she arrived in China. Nor did it end almost forty years later when her spirit departed her frail, emaciated body on a ship in the harbor of Kobe, Japan. The journey continues today in the lives of those who respond to God's call to share the gospel in foreign lands. It is a journey of faith and sacrifice.

Missionaries arrive on foreign fields and feel overwhelmed by spiritual darkness and the condition of people locked into traditional cultures and religious superstitions. Opportunities for service and witness seem to multiply uncontrollably, and resources seem so limited. Lottie Moon is renowned not only for what she did in China, but also for her resounding call for Southern Baptists to become a missions people and respond to those opportunities.

As our trip came to an end, I left China with a deeper respect and gratitude for her steadfastness in confronting tradition, for her unsurpassed love of the Chinese people, and for her compulsion to exalt her Savior to the ends of the earth. I understood more fully the implications of her determination to challenge those at home to join in the task of reaching the lost through their prayers, financial support, and sending laborers into the field. I was refreshed, renewed, and resolved to face the future with confidence that Southern Baptists will respond to the missions challenge today as they did in an era now past.

The journey will not end until Christ comes again. Lottie Moon continues to be the banner that rallies us to faithfulness and keeps us moving forward in confidence of victory, fulfilling the mission God has given us. She once said, "I have a firm conviction that I am immortal till my work is done."[5] Retracing Lottie's steps became a pilgrimage that brought my own call into new perspective. It renewed my vision of what God is doing in our world and the unprecedented missions opportunity before us, a task that is immortal until finished.

The first step in this journey, however, began in central Virginia as I gazed over the rolling hills Lottie knew as her home. ❧

Some of the fields and streams from Lottie Moon's childhood still stand untouched by the years near Charlottesville, Virginia. A lively and active child like Lottie had great places to run and play, or sit quietly and reflect.

Every morning, field workers outside the Chinese village of Shaling trudge up this road to work. One of Lottie Moon's earliest works was in this area, Pingtu Province. Scenes like this have changed little in the decades since she was here.

Today's rural China would look very familiar to Lottie Moon, were she still alive to see scenes like these field workers going home after a day of hard labor. Walking and bicycle-riding are the most typical ways of getting around. In her travels around the provinces, she saw many such sundowns and shared the road with walkers, animals, sedan chairs, and bicycle riders.

If there had been a nursery at the Fourth Pingdu Church in the early 1900s, these members would have been the bed babies and toddlers. Generations of faithful believers remind us that the Lord, who used servants like Lottie Moon and others in this part of China years ago, does begin good work and sees it to completion.

Traditional Chinese architecture has stories to tell. Pitched-tile roofs often have human, animal, and mythical figures along the edges and at the corners. Some Chinese believed the figures could protect the building against bad omens and evil spirits.

China is an increasingly industrialized society, with factories like this one near Yantai working to produce the energy and goods necessary for a nation of more than a billion people.

The real "monuments" of Monument Street Church in Tengchow are the faithful believers who are still there after scores of years and the ups and downs of everyday life. Rather than the traditional good luck symbols found on ancient Chinese roofs, church members chose to put a simple cross.

Having a Bible and a church open for prayer and worship are treasures for believers everywhere. Hong En He, a member of Monument Street Church in Tengchow, enjoys such a moment in the sanctuary of her church. Her husband, Qui Jai Ye, is pastor of the church.

In Albemarle County, Virginia, during Lottie Moon's growing up years, home and family—some dating back many generations—were revered. There would have been little chance to "think globally" in such an atmosphere. But becoming a worker for Christ, Lottie caught a vision for the world beyond the familiar boundaries of her childhood universe.

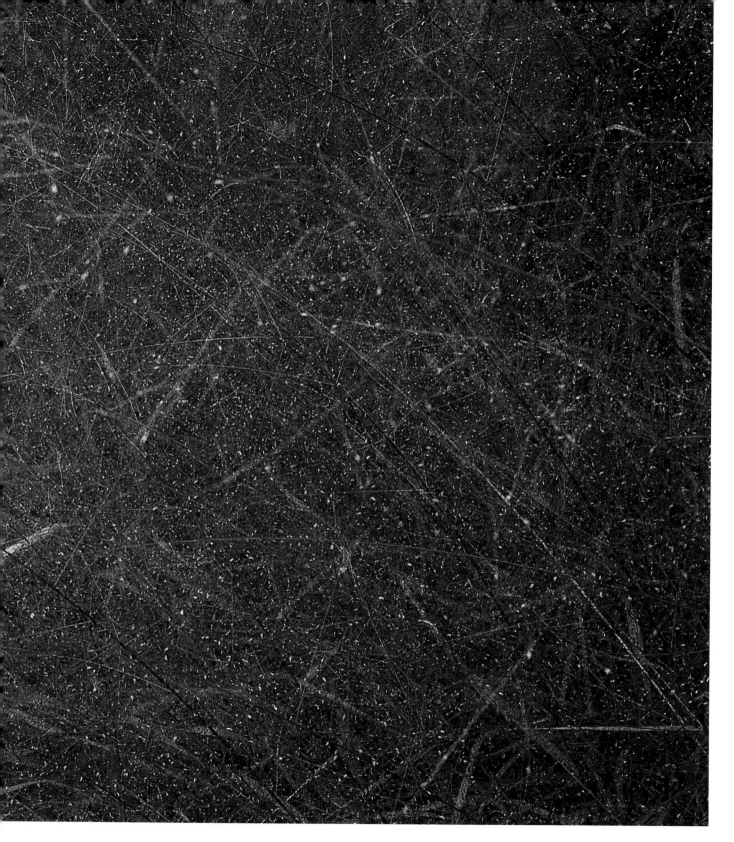

🕊️ 'Once the Lord entered her life, His divine plan began to unfold in a way that would change the course of missions for generations to come. God used Lottie Moon to proclaim to the people of north China the good news of Jesus Christ.'

—Jerry Rankin

*Above: **Home from teaching in Danville, Kentucky, in the summer of 1870, thirty-year-old Lottie shared her interest in missions service with sister Edmonia.***

*Left: **Lottie Moon was one of seven brothers and sisters who grew up on the Viewmont estate near Thomas Jefferson's Monticello in Albemarle County, Virginia. Foreign Mission Board President Jerry Rankin surveys Viewmont as it looks today.***

A few miles outside Charlottesville, Virginia, we exited Interstate 64 and drove a short distance on State Highway 80 toward Scottsville. There we stopped and gazed over a long board fence that framed an expanse of green, rolling hills. This was Viewmont, the plantation where Charlotte Digges Moon was born in 1840, the place she called home for much of her life.

The original buildings are gone now, but pictures from the era show what the setting of Lottie's life in nineteenth century America looked like. Her father was a wealthy landowner who provided Lottie, her mother, and her six siblings with the privileges of prosperity in the young American republic. Edward Moon owned 1,500 acres in this part of Albemarle County.

Surveying the lush meadows and vales, I could envision the young Lottie playing with her siblings and cousins on

the clover-covered hillsides. As I reflected on her later self-imposed poverty in China, I wondered how often she must have thought back to those carefree days of luxury and comfort, gaiety and social life at Viewmont.

The Moon home was a prominent center of entertainment as well as hospitable respite for prominent visitors. From the vantage point on the hill of their appropriately named estate, the family could observe guests arriving long before they turned horse and buggy off the main road onto the tree-lined lane approaching the house.

Even the tragedy of losing her father did not destroy Lottie's early happiness and affluence. After he died in a riverboat accident on the Mississippi in January 1853, Lottie's mother, Anna Maria Moon, worked diligently to keep the family fortune intact. In a family of less substantial means, someone of Lottie's age would have been expected to help rear the younger children or work to help support the family. But Anna Maria Moon had different expectations.

At age fourteen, Lottie enrolled in the Virginia Female Seminary (which became Hollins College). She excelled in her studies and graduated in 1856. Her family expectations for education were high, so she enrolled in the Albemarle Female Institute in Charlottesville. She quickly plunged into the study of classic and modern languages. In four years she received both undergraduate and graduate degrees.

While blooming socially and academically, Lottie was slow to develop the spiritual side of her life. She was outspoken in her disinterest in organized religion and sometimes irreverent in her attitude. That began to change after she entered Albemarle Institute and started attending First Baptist Church of Charlottesville, whose pastor was the legendary John A. Broadus.

Her original motives for attending worship services at

ness as she pursued her academic work. Her mischievousness began to fade. Her earlier religious doubts never again surfaced as she gave herself earnestly to a higher calling. Once the Lord entered her life, His divine plan began to unfold in a way that would change the course of missions for generations to come. God used Lottie Moon to proclaim to the people of north China the good news of Jesus Christ. But He also used her life and work to inspire thousands of others to follow her into selfless living among people in faraway places. She, who had known wealth in America, lived on a pittance in China. At the end of her life she gave away to others what little she had until she began to starve. And in death she gave to many, many others the vision of what it truly means to follow God wherever He leads.

I have been amazed to find that with each experience of growth in grace, one becomes aware of a need to know more of Jesus. Every blessing and taste of His power creates a deeper hunger and thirst for more of His righteousness. To experience His touch is to be made aware of the ugliness of our sin and the ever-present power of the flesh. But change comes when one comes to Jesus in repentance and faith, and the regenerating power of the Holy Spirit begins to produce a vessel fit for the Master's service.

Lottie's walk with our Lord began with her conversion at First Baptist Church in Charlottesville. Fifteen years later,

Far left: **Hardware (formerly Pine Grove) Baptist Church was one of two churches Lottie Moon's mother attended with her children. Lottie joined the church by letter in 1862 and taught Sunday School there.**

Left: **Inside the church, Rankin examines a plaque commemorating Lottie's membership and service.**

First Baptist remain unclear, but the results are indisputable. Either Broadus' strong personality or his intellectual powers broke through the hard shell of skepticism that had kept Lottie from a personal relationship with Jesus Christ. On December 21, 1858, Lottie responded to an altar call during a revival service and committed her life to Christ.

That experience immediately changed Lottie's life and demeanor. She studied the Scriptures with as much earnest-

The familiar fields, ridges and farm sights and smells around Viewmont were always home to Lottie Moon, but she spent little time here after she left America for China. In those days, missionaries quite often left thinking they would never see home or loved ones again on earth.

'…,[S]ome things remain constant. People in China, and all around the world, still need Jesus. Missionaries continue to struggle under their load and plead for reinforcements to join them in answering the call. The Lottie Moon Christmas Offering and the Cooperative Program continue to support the sending of missionaries and reaching our world. And the Woman's Missionary Union continues a journey of faith and sacrifice to serve the cause of missions.'

—Jerry Rankin

> ❧ 'Christ uses our lives for His divine purposes. For some, that means leaving familiar environments and comforts to share the good news of God's love with those who would not otherwise have the opportunity to hear.'
>
> —*Jerry Rankin*

God led her to leave her promising teaching career and answer His call to the mission field. Her dedication was never questioned, but her challenges were numerous. Like many who follow in her steps today, she arrived on the field and became caught up in the demands and problems of daily life as a missionary—administrative responsibility, interpersonal conflicts, cross-cultural tensions—all of which allow our all-too-human nature to show.

When Lottie began to visit the villages of China, however, she discovered the joy of telling spiritually hungry people about Jesus. This seemed to propel her toward a new dimension of fellowship with the Lord. Concern for personal comforts and needs seemed to diminish almost entirely in her later years. She would paraphrase the apostle Paul and say, "I hold not my life of any account as dear unto myself, that I may accomplish my course."[1]

I count myself among those influenced by Lottie's life. When I seek to explain my own call to missions, many impressions and experiences come to mind. The beginning of my call started when, as a ten-year-old boy, I accepted Jesus Christ as my personal Lord and Savior. When I opened my heart to trust Jesus, I knew that my sins had been forgiven and I had been reconciled to God for all eternity. I will never forget how joy and peace flooded my heart. I remember thinking, "I wish all the people in the world could have the joy and assurance of knowing Jesus." Later, inspiring speakers at missions conferences and revivals stirred me to surrender and commit my life to God's divine plan. Mission trips in college helped affirm that calling.

As a ten-year-old, I did not realize where God would lead me. As an eighteen-year-old new believer, Lottie could not have anticipated what God would do with her life, either. But once we belong to Him, Christ uses our lives for His divine purposes. For some, that means leaving familiar environments and comforts to share the good news of God's love with those who would not otherwise have the opportunity to hear.

Lottie went to serve in a part of the world where few people had heard about God's love in Jesus Christ. Even though she was eighteen when she accepted Christ into her heart, Lottie grew up in an environment where Christ was

*Far left: **A blue daisy at Viewmont, Lottie's birthplace, greets tiny visitors. Lottie planted bits of Virginia along the walkway of her Tengchow residence—crape myrtle, touch-me-nots, hollyhocks, verbena and roses.***

*Left: **Rankin pauses at the plaque which identifies Lottie Moon's birthplace. The plaque was a gift of Woman's Missionary Union, Albemarle Baptist Association of Virginia.***

preached. Her father accepted Christ into his heart shortly before Lottie was born, thanks to the witness and influence of Lottie's mother. The Moon family attended the Baptist church in nearby Scottsville. Her father had made a large contribution to the construction of that church in 1842.

That church building is still in use today—the U-shaped slave balcony betraying its pre-Civil War design despite periodic renovation. Also on display behind the pulpit, and on each side, are the sofa and two chairs donated from the Moon home.

Her mother valiantly held on to Viewmont after her husband's death and the Civil War, but the Moon children eventually sold the plantation piece by piece. The family scattered, but Lottie's sister Edmonia returned from her missionary service in China to purchase a little cottage in Scottsville. Her older sister, Orianna, a physician, later returned to practice medicine in Scottsville and is buried in the local cemetery. Scottsville was Lottie's furlough home during her earlier times of returning to the United States. She joined the Woman's Missionary Union there before her return to China in 1893.

Another important place in the Moon family's life was the Hardware Baptist Church, situated about four miles from Viewmont. When we visited that little white clapboard

Above right: **Like fall color, Lottie's legacy and inspiration are celebrated each year.**

Below right: **Rankin strolls past the sentry-like columns of Scottsville (Va.) Baptist Church. Lottie's parents helped erect the building in 1842. Many of the Moon family's finishing touches have been preserved.**

Center: **Rankin speaks inside the Scottsville church, where Lottie's parents were members. The chairs on the platform came from the Moon estate.**

Far right: **A visitor is shown in silhouette through a church window donated by Lottie's parents.**

church in the middle of a clearing, I smelled the nostalgic aroma of a wood stove still used in the Sunday School rooms behind the auditorium. The church began as Pine Grove Baptist Church in 1802 but later moved to its present location by the Hardware Creek. When Lottie finished school at Albemarle Female Institute, she returned home to Viewmont to help her mother protect the plantation from the ravages of the Civil War era. The remaining family members had moved their membership to this nearby community church, and Lottie joined too. She was a devout church member, serving as a Sunday School teacher.

 'If she had been thinking of the country she had left, she would have had the opportunity to return. Instead, she was longing for a better country— a heavenly one. Therefore, God is not ashamed to be called her God, for He has prepared a city for her.'

—Hebrews 11:15-16 (paraphrased)

Lottie came was not important; it was the quality of her commitment that counted. The same holds true for our missionaries today. Our Lord said, "He who is faithful in a very little thing is faithful also in much" (Luke 16:10). When she was a member of this small, rural church, Lottie Moon did not realize that God would use her in such great and significant ways. But she was faithful in the opportunity she had at the time.

Lottie left home in 1863 and began tutoring the children of well-to-do families in South Carolina, Georgia, and Alabama. She kept only what she needed to live on and sent the rest of her pay to her mother. During this time Lottie not only learned a pattern of personal sacrifice for others, but she also experienced teaching—a skill that equipped her for the ministry to which God would call her in China.

Missionaries have not been allowed in China for many years, but we can go there to teach. In an effort to join the

When we visited the church, a couple of pews sat on the raised platform to the left of the pulpit, facing the congregation. In this "choir" section, Lottie Moon would teach her Sunday School class each Sunday morning. A small plaque on the wall commemorated the few years her spiritual journey led her through the fellowship of this little church.

How significant that Southern Baptists' most renowned missionary would claim an identity with a church so representative of our rural heritage! Hardware Church is so much like many of our nearly 40,000 Southern Baptist congregations today. The size of the church from which

Above: **John A. Broadus, pastor of First Baptist Church in Charlottesville, Virginia, was holding a series of evangelistic meetings there at the time Lottie made public her profession of faith in Christ on December 21, 1858.**

Right: **First Baptist Church in Charlottesville as it appeared during Lottie's young life.**

Far right: **Church and family members look on with pride as new missionaries share their personal testimonies during a 1982 appointment service inside the church. Since Lottie Moon's missionary appointment on July 7, 1873, about 12,000 Southern Baptist missionaries have been appointed.**

global community, China has opened its doors to foreigners who are willing to teach there. Each year hundreds of Southern Baptists—not necessarily those with theological educations and pastoral experience, but those with professional experience as teachers, technicians, and business people—follow in Lottie's steps as teachers in this vast country where so many still need to hear of God's love in Christ. These Christian teachers have the opportunity to live out their faith in China by teaching in that nation's 1,075 colleges and universities.[2] Americans are responding to only a fraction of the requests for them to teach English in China.

I pray that many Southern Baptists who may not be on the traditional "missionary" track of calling and preparation would make themselves available to God's leadership and respond to other opportunities to follow in Lottie's steps. She diligently pursued the educational opportunities provided to

her. She faithfully developed and used her skills wherever she was. Lottie did all this unaware that God was preparing her for a task that would advance His kingdom beyond her wildest dreams.

'He who is faithful in a very little thing is faithful also in much.'

—Luke 16:10

'*How many members are being called out to missionary service? That is the evidence of a church that takes the Great Commission seriously.*'

—*Jerry Rankin*

CHAPTER TWO

Almost 100 years after Lottie Moon boarded the *Costa Rica* in the San Francisco harbor bound for China, my wife, Bobbye, and I, along with our two-year-old daughter, Lori, and ten-month-old son, Russell, boarded the S.S. *President Cleveland* for the transpacific cruise to the Orient.

Bobbye felt the same sense of calling to the mission that lay before us as I did. Her involvement in Girls in Action as a child had given her an impression that God wanted her to be a missionary someday. That impression, reinforced by friends and encouraged by the leadership of the rural, south Mississippi church she grew up in, resulted in a deep spiritual commitment. It was during a missions conference while a student at Mississippi College that God's call was confirmed, and God brought our lives together with a vision to serve Him overseas.

We were among the last of the "boat people," as younger

Lottie Moon's first missionary journey to China began in August 1873. From this train station in Cartersville, Georgia, Lottie made her way to San Francisco. There she received word that the Woman's Missionary Society in Cartersville planned to support her.

*Right top: **Lottie Moon and Anna Safford lived in this house while teaching in Cartersville, Georgia. Anna Safford (woman's portrait), a good friend of Lottie Moon's, taught with her at the Caldwell Institute in Danville, Kentucky. With churches still uneasy about appointing single female missionaries, the two later carved out their own niches as principals of the Cartersville (Georgia) Female High School. Anna became a Presbyterian missionary to China.***

*Center: **An antique-store window in Scottsville, Virginia, reflects the steeple and cross on Scottsville United Methodist Church, where James Barclay, Lottie Moon's uncle, attended at the time he became a missionary with the Disciples of Christ.***

missionaries now refer to those of us who went to the field in the era of ship travel. Thanks to modern jets, new missionaries today are thrust into the cacophony of sounds and strange sights of a foreign culture in a matter of hours.

The comforts of our modern ship differed considerably from those available on

PRESBYTERIAN CHURCH (USA)

Lottie's five-week voyage. In February 1971, we said goodbye to a large gathering of relatives at the airport in Jackson, Mississippi. Tears flowed, but the sadness of separation melted into the joy of fulfilling a divine calling. Our parents would have preferred that we remain in Mississippi and serve the Lord in a nearby pastorate so they could enjoy their grandchildren. Their normal desire, however, was overwhelmed by their eagerness for us to obey God's will.

We left Mississippi on a snowy winter day, and left our winter coats and gloves with friends in California, who mailed them back to Mississippi. Three other new Southern Baptist missionary families joined us on the ship bound for tropical Indonesia: Jerry and Elaine Perrill, Murphy and Linda Terry,

who were planning to open Southern Baptist work in Laos, and Lehman and Virginia Webb, en route to Singapore. Other missionaries of various denominations also were on board. We experienced wonderful fellowship with all of them. Unlike Lottie's storm-tossed adventure, we had a relaxed time, despite occasional seasickness.

In September 1873, Lottie also joined a large group of missionaries going to the Orient. For her, as for other Southern

cisco Bay never expecting to return home. In 1971, we were counting the days, anticipating our first furlough, seeing friends and loved ones four years later. There was no such anticipation in Lottie's day. The length and difficulty of overseas travel made return trips impractical. Travel to the mission field was a one-way ticket. Moreover, nineteenth-century missionaries believed relationships with people overseas could be built only by burning bridges that led back home and planting their lives on foreign soil until death. Crowds would gather at departure times for new missionaries and sing *God Be with You Till We Meet Again*—presumably in heaven.

I can only imagine the emotions Lottie, then thirty-two, felt as she listened to that song at her departure. She knew she would see her sister Edmonia, who had gone to China more than a year earlier. But she was leaving behind other family members who had scattered after her mother's death in 1870.

In many ways, Lottie's departure for China began much earlier, when she received her call to mission service during the two years she was teaching in Cartersville, Georgia. She had moved there from Danville, Kentucky, where she also had taught. She went to Cartersville at the request of a cousin who lived in the community. He and other local businessmen recognized the need for a school for children there. Lottie's good friend and colleague Anna Safford, a Presbyterian,

Baptists in her day, foreign missions was a relatively new pursuit. The orientation and preparation we provide for new missionaries today was not available to Lottie and her peers. Once the Foreign Mission Board approved her appointment, she moved rather rapidly to get on the field. She passed through Virginia for a quick farewell to relatives, then boarded a train in Baltimore to begin the journey.

Lottie and other missionaries in 1873 departed San Fran-

James Barclay, traveled to Judea in 1850 as the first missionary of the Disciples of Christ. His work certainly received the attention of his young niece, Lottie.

helped her manage the Cartersville school.

What exactly led to Lottie's call remains uncertain. Her uncle, James Barclay, traveled to Judea in 1850 as the first missionary of the Disciples of Christ. His work certainly received Lottie's family's attention. Living in the South and attending a Southern Baptist church provided her with knowledge about the new Southern Baptist Convention's strong commitment to foreign missions. Accounts of the lives of some of the fledgling denomination's missionaries already were appearing in publications.

She likely discussed the possibility of missionary service with her friend Anna, who also left the Cartersville school to go to China with the Presbyterians. Both women had a keen interest in overseas work and recognized the importance of a God-centered education. Although the school at Cartersville was nondenominational, they included Bible study in the curriculum. Lottie taught the younger children and Anna the older ones.

Before going to China, Lottie and her sister Edmonia made significant financial contributions to the Foreign Mission Board's work in China. I doubt, however, that she initially thought of being more than a financial and prayer supporter of the missionaries. The Foreign Mission Board, under the leadership of James B. Taylor, was not considering the appointment of single women at the time, especially after the unfortunate

failure of such an effort in 1853. That position changed after Taylor's death in 1871. Henry Allen Tupper was elected corresponding secretary of the board in 1872. Under his leadership the Foreign Mission Board recognized the potential of missionary women to meet the vast, unmet needs of women and children in China.

Lottie's sister Edmonia quickly sought appointment and received board endorsement in April 1872. Seeing her younger sister embark on a pioneering role that more befitted Lottie might have sparked the sense of challenge and adventure to which she always responded.

Regardless of other factors, God used the preaching of R.B. Headden, Lottie's pastor at Cartersville, to impress upon her a specific, personal missions call. He had attended an associational meeting at which pastors were encouraged to preach on foreign missions. The following Sunday, in February 1873, he made an impassioned appeal for a greater concern for the lost in pagan lands and the need for laborers. All the impressions and influences nudging Lottie's life toward missions came into focus at that moment. She spent the afternoon in contemplation and prayer to resolve the issue once and for all. The day concluded with a firm commitment to God's call to China.

Many pastors claim an exemption from missionary service on the basis of a call to build and nurture the home support base for foreign missions. That is certainly needed. But as I travel about the United States, I see numerous churches even in smaller towns and communities. It's difficult for me to accept the proposition that perhaps 95 percent of those who have been called to proclaim the gospel should seek to minister to less than 5 percent of the world's population living in the United States—where access to the good news of salvation is readily available.

My convictions were influenced by the persuasive preaching of Baker James Cauthen. During the 25 years Dr. Cauthen served as president of the Foreign Mission Board, he challenged pastors to consider the needs of a lost world. Though health factors and other circumstances would divert many from missionary appointment, he insisted that everyone should surrender and be willing to go until God closes the door.

Pastors often become preoccupied with building only a local ministry and lose the biblical perspective of reaching the world. If God has ratified a pastor's assignment at home, then there should be those—like Lottie—who are being called to missions through the pastor's passion and burden for making Christ known to the world.

A pastor of a large church shared with me his pride in leading his missions-minded congregation. He alluded to the generous missions offering given each year and the impressive number of church volunteers participating in missions projects.

I was truly impressed and expressed appreciation, but asked, "How many members are being called out to missionary service?" That is the evidence of a church that takes the Great Commission seriously. That response affirms a pastor's heart crying for the numberless millions who have no opportunity to hear and respond to the gospel.

If the thousands of pastors who stay at home and minister to churches would truly become a base for reaching the world, they would not simply draw a circle around their community and rationalize that as their part in fulfilling the Great Commission. They would be mobilizing prayer for the nations and unreached people groups, preaching missions with a passion from the heart of God, and—like R.B. Headden exhorting Lottie Moon—challenging members to sacrificial surrender to missionary service.

Lottie had earlier begun corresponding with Henry Allen Tupper at the Foreign Mission Board, but their communication intensified as she began to anticipate joining Edmonia in China. At a time when few people, especially single women, ventured beyond the country where they were born, the proposition of spending a lifetime in China reflected somewhat radical thinking. But with the support of Tupper and the endorsement of the Foreign Mission Board, the pioneering spirits of Edmonia and Lottie Moon were quickly emulated by other women who made themselves available for overseas service.

'… her dedication and acceptance of her Master's call on her life provided her with a singular purpose in life. Her devotion to the Word of God and sound doctrine was an essential ingredient in her spiritual impact on a lost nation.'

—Jerry Rankin

'Join with me in suffering for the gospel according to the power of God; who has saved us, and called us with a holy calling, not according to our works, but according to His own purpose and grace which was granted us in Christ Jesus from all eternity.'

—II Timothy 1:8b-9

The ranks of single women on the foreign mission field increased and still represent a valuable segment of the more than 4,000 Southern Baptist missionaries under assignment today.

In just the last year of appointments—544 missions workers were appointed by the Foreign Mission Board in 1995 [1] —single women were assigned to almost every conceivable type of ministry. Some went as teachers—even to China, like Lottie. Others accepted positions as theological educators,

Far left: **The 150th anniversary of the Foreign Mission Board was celebrated in May 1995 at the board's home office in Richmond, Virginia. Those who attended were greeted by a banner imprinted with the board's mission statement.**

Above left: **Participants in the celebration fill the Baker James Cauthen Chapel of the Foreign Mission Board.**

Below left: **At the conclusion of the festivities, Eloise Glass Cauthen (l) chats with Alice Gaventa, retired missionary to Nigeria, and Kathryn Bullard, former Woman's Missionary Union executive director for Virginia. Mrs. Cauthen, now deceased, was a missionary to China and wife of the late Baker James Cauthen, executive director of the Foreign Mission Board from 1954 to 1979.**

doctors, agriculturists, and mission business managers. Recognizing the initial breakthrough to starting a church can come through children's and women's community ministries, some women missionaries went out as church planters and developers to work with overseas pastors and missionary colleagues. Still others went as strategy coordinators assigned to devise plans for reaching unevangelized people groups.

We make a greater impact on the lost world when we

> ❧ *'Those [Chinese] long forbidden to worship publicly, along with new Christians who had only recently discovered the living Savior, now stood together in awe of a mighty God on the throne of grace. God truly inhabits the praises of His people.'*
>
> —*Jerry Rankin*

recognize the potential calling and divine gifts of *all* those in the Body of Christ, including dedicated women, both married and single. The place of women in ministry was as controversial a century ago as it is today, and Lottie Moon was one of the strongest advocates that women be fully utilized in the ministry of the church. However, she qualified this clearly in a letter to the *Religious Herald*, Virginia Baptists' newspaper, in 1871. "Our Lord does not call on women to preach, or to pray in public, but no less does He say to them than to men, 'Go work today in My vineyard.' "[2] Even as she later shared the gospel among the villages and in homes in China, she would exclude men from the room, and was most uncomfortable when they would slip in the door to hear her words of evangelistic witness.

Once they had made their missionary commitment and the school year had ended, Lottie and Anna Safford resigned their positions at the Cartersville school and began preparing for appointment to China, each with their separate mission boards. The women of First Baptist Church in Cartersville mobilized to support Lottie, and immediately after her appointment organized the first Woman's Missionary Society among Georgia Baptists.[3]

Along with Dellanna O'Brien, executive director of the Southern Baptist Woman's Missionary Union, I visited the original church building where Lottie made her missions com-

mitment and the Woman's Missionary Society was formed. After the church moved, the building was turned into an apartment. A young couple recently purchased the building to turn it into a home. A plaque in front of the building commemorates its historic significance to Southern Baptists. Dr. O'Brien and I drove from the church to the train station where Lottie said her goodbyes en route to Virginia and on to China.

In Lottie's day—and to a certain extent in our own—it was sometimes presumed that an unmarried person who left for the mission field would remain single. Some today never give serious consideration to the prospects of marriage and family as they pursue their missions call. Others struggle with the seeming permanence of their single status, even overseas.

Little is known of Lottie Moon's social life, or whether suitors expressed an interest in her. Schooling at institutions exclusively for girls, the isolation at Viewmont, and the trauma of the Civil War, as well as the strict social mores of the day, would not have enhanced the prospects for developing a relationship with male acquaintances who measured up to Lottie's standards of intellect and piety. However, historians theorize about her attraction to a young professor who split his teaching between the University of Virginia and the Albemarle Female Institute in Charlottesville. Dr. Crawford Toy and Lottie maintained regular correspondence over the years, and the legend persists that a romantic attraction drew the two to each other. Few people could match Lottie's intelligence and wit, and the professor must have been impressed with her understanding of his lessons and flattered by her personal interest.

Even after her arrival in China, Lottie wrote home suggesting a possible resignation and hinting that preparations should be made for a wedding. However, no mention is made of the relationship later after Toy was dismissed from the faculty of Southern Baptist Theological Seminary in Louisville, Kentucky, in 1879 for views that were perceived to be inconsistent with Southern Baptist theology. Toy had been educated in the German school of "higher criticism" of the Bible and apparently questioned the authority and reliability of Scripture as accepted by the churches of the denomination. His views became evident when he later became a Unitarian. Lottie may have recognized the incompatibility of his teaching with a basic doctrine of her faith: that all who have yet to come to repentance and faith in Jesus Christ are lost, whether in China or America.

A review of history reveals that Southern Baptists have always championed the infallible Word of God as the sole authority for all matters of faith and practice. Once that authority is questioned or compromised, the foundation of one's faith becomes subject to every whim of belief and human doctrine. When two prominent pastors submitted themselves for appointment by the Foreign Mission Board in 1881, they were appointed, but their appointments were later withdrawn because they refused to subscribe to the verbal, plenary inspiration of the Scripture. The board affirmed the priesthood of all believers and their prerogative to hold to their own views, but said it would be inappropriate to appoint and support missionaries whose beliefs do not represent those of their Southern Baptist constituency.

Historians don't know if theological differences brought an end to the Lottie Moon-Crawford Toy relationship. We do know her dedication and acceptance of her Master's call on her life provided her with a singular purpose in life. Her devotion to the Word of God and sound doctrine was an essential ingredient in her spiritual impact on a lost nation.

Today, the Foreign Mission Board emphasizes the need to evangelize people groups who have never heard the gospel of Jesus Christ preached. When I identify and describe some of these unreached people groups in the Muslim world or former communist countries, I emphasize the need for us to proclaim the gospel as the only hope of salvation. Confronted with the reality of multitudes who live entire lifetimes following the traditions and religions of their cultures, never having the opportunity to hear of Jesus Christ, some will say, "Surely a loving and merciful God would not condemn people to hell if they have never had a chance to be saved!" I cringe at these

words, because they represent a not-so-subtle form of universalism that is creeping into the thinking of many Christians. They are yielding to their own rationalizations rather than the clear, authoritative teaching of God's Word.

The Bible says "all have sinned and fall short of the glory of God" (Rom. 3:23). God does not condemn those who have never heard the gospel—those 1.7 billion people today who have yet to hear the name of Jesus and be given an opportunity to be saved.

They are condemned by their own sin, for all have sinned. Sin separates all people from God, and the only possibility of reconciliation with God is through His provision of salvation in the redeeming death and resurrection of Jesus Christ.

If there were any possibility people who have never heard could be saved due to their ignorance, then our most effective mission strategy would be silence. We should determine never to mention the name of Jesus lest those who have never heard would then hear and be accountable and condemned. But the Bible doesn't tell us to be silent. God's Word makes no allowance for those who have not heard. Jesus said, "I am the way, and the truth, and the life; no one comes to the Father, but through Me" (John 14:6). That's why we are told, "Go into all the world and preach the gospel to all creation" (Mark 16:1). There is no other provision or hope except in Jesus Christ.

Lottie Moon believed this beyond the shadow of a doubt.

*Above, far left: **Cartersville (Georgia) Baptist Church located on Market Street (now Cherokee Avenue) as it looked in 1903.***

*Below, far left: **Dellanna O'Brien, executive director of the Woman's Missionary Union, and Rankin look at a monument recalling Lottie Moon's surrender to missions at the original site of the Cartersville Baptist Church. The monument honors Moon as a "gifted educator, promoter of world missions, committed evangelist, devoted minister of the gospel."***

*Left: **The building where the church met in Lottie's time is now privately owned. The congregation, renamed First Baptist Church, now meets a few blocks away, continuing to shed light on its surrounding community and the world.***

As I studied her letters and writings it became clear to me that they reflected a well-defined theology. To ignore her views in this area is to miss a significant and important part of her personality and faith.

As she considered nineteenth-century China, an ancient civilization yet to emerge into the modern world, without the benefit of spiritual enlightenment of the truth of Jesus Christ, her heart groaned. She grieved to think of the lost souls entering a Christless eternity, simply because so few had gone to tell them the story of Jesus.

I will never forget the thrill of anticipation that filled my heart as we left for Indonesia. I had been richly blessed to live in a country where I could hear of Jesus and come to know Him personally at an early age. I did not deserve the mercies of God that allowed me to be born into a Christian family and nurtured by a loving church fellowship. And now I had received the joy and privilege of introducing my Savior, the Light of the world, to those in the largest Muslim nation in the world.

I am sure Lottie, like all the missionaries I have known, felt those same emotions as she boarded the train in Cartersville, and later set sail from San Francisco. She no doubt experienced anxiety about the unknown, the loneliness, the hardships she would face. But that was overcome by the anticipation of bringing the light of Jesus Christ to the darkness in the hearts of the Chinese people.

Right: **The ancient water gate to Tengchow (now Penglai), along with the wall, defended the city from pirates and marauders. In the distance is the beach where Lottie Moon and her fellow missionaries celebrated the Fourth of July.**

Far right: **Henry Allen Tupper was elected corresponding secretary (president) of the Foreign Mission Board in 1872. Under his leadership the board recognized the potential of missionary women like Lottie Moon to meet the vast, unmet needs of women and children in China.**

The indomitable Lottie grimly endured seasickness during most of her five-week ocean voyage from San Francisco to China. Her ship stopped briefly in Yokohama, Japan. So did ours in 1971. That first exposure to the multitudes of the Orient gave Lottie—and us—a glimpse of the environment for missionary work in that part of the world.

Lottie disembarked at Shanghai, China, on October 7, 1873. She was welcomed by missionaries Matthew and Eliza Yates and T.P. and Martha Crawford. The largest city and primary port of entry for China, Shanghai today has a population of more than 13 million people. I imagine that Lottie's arrival there, almost a century earlier, was not unlike ours in Jakarta, the capital and port city of Indonesia. With 7 million people, and yet to enter an era of rapid development and modernization, Jakarta overwhelmed us with sights and sounds.

Yet as we made our way through the endless maze of

> ❧ *'Because the Holy Spirit indwells the message of the gospel, it is the power of God unto salvation. How faithful and diligent we must be to proclaim it and allow it to do its work of grace in the hearts of the lost.'*
>
> —*Jerry Rankin*

❧ 'The Red Guards, while successful in closing [the church's] doors for a brief period during the Cultural Revolution, could not silence the faithful preaching of Jesus Christ and Him crucified.'

—Jerry Rankin

Street vendors bundle against the chill in Yantai. The city, previously known as Chefoo, was the site of Lottie's arrival in North China.

narrow, potholed streets, we felt the darkness—literally and figuratively. The few street lights glowed dimly, and the flickering fires beside the roadway barely illuminated the shadowy silhouettes of hawkers peddling their wares. We were thankful for the missionaries who met us and provided a sense of security in that unfamiliar environment.

When Lottie arrived in China, the Yateses had already served in Shanghai for twenty-seven years. A legendary pioneer in foreign missions, Matthew Yates served in China for forty-two years. The Crawfords, who became Lottie's colleagues in North China, had been appointed in 1851. The pattern of Southern Baptist work for its first century in China was being established with the South China Mission, centered in Canton. The Central China Mission worked inland from Shanghai, and the North China Mission launched work into Shantung Province from Tengchow.

Edmonia Moon had stayed behind in Tengchow to prepare for her sister's arrival, so Lottie was impatient to get there. She and Martha Crawford sailed to Chefoo (now called Yantai), the main seaport on the Shantung Peninsula. After meeting missionary J.B. Hartwell, they traveled by *shentze*—a small covered compartment on two long wooden poles, borne in front and behind by horses or coolies—to Tengchow, sixty miles up the coast. Our journey to this area of China, more than a century later, was considerably easier. We flew in a

comfortable plane from China's capital, Beijing, to the modern city of Yantai in less than an hour. Then we retraced Lottie's route, which took her two days, in a mere hour and a half by air-conditioned bus.

Shandong Province, as it is called today, lacks the bustle of Shanghai or Beijing, the relics of Xian, or the economic development of Guangzhou (Canton) that commend those areas to tourists. Terraced hillsides and wheat fields extend all along the road—reflecting the agrarian economy of the area. Shandong sits in approximately the same latitude as Virginia, so Lottie must have welcomed the familiar climate and seasonal changes.

The inner city is still known as Chefoo, but the larger metropolitan area known as Yantai now is home to more than 6 million people. The early Presbyterian mission had centered its work there, so the Baptists (with the exception of Hartwell) moved up the coast to Tengchow, or Penglai as it is called today. Our hotel overlooked the harbor where Lottie's ship arrived from Shanghai. The lighthouse from that era still shines on the rocky coastal entry into the port.

Shantung Province was the most populous in China a century ago, and the American consulate operated in Chefoo. The buildings of the Chefoo School, where "missionary kids" from throughout North China came for boarding, remain in excellent repair, and are used today as a naval academy. The

*Right: **A monument built by an ancient warlord and placed in honor of his parents designates Monument Street in Tengchow.***

*Above, far right: **"The house at the Little Crossroads" was one of several residences occupied by Lottie Moon in China.***

*Below, far right: **The Rankins and Pastor Qin Jai Ye talk with children outside Monument Street Church, founded by T.P. and Martha Crawford—two of Lottie's fellow workers.***

school is now located in Malaysia, and I have visited many times there. I never dreamed I would see the original campus in what is now Yantai.

We arrived in Yantai on Saturday afternoon and hurried to Penglai, Lottie's home and headquarters for her thirty-nine years in China. At the turn of the century it thrived as a center of commerce with a population of 80,000. Today, despite the modernization of much of its industry, the city's population barely tops 100,000—a medium-sized town by modern Chinese standards. There Lottie immersed herself in learning the difficult tonal language and adapting to Chinese culture. She joined Edmonia in boarding with the Crawfords. In that day, single missionaries were expected to live with other families and work under the direction and authority of the senior missionary.

Lottie almost immediately started writing to Henry Allen Tupper at the Foreign Mission Board in Richmond, seeking her own home. Several years later she moved into what she called "the house at the Little Crossroads." Historians are unable to pinpoint the exact house where Lottie lived, so we don't know if it is still standing. However, they have identified the area and a house that may have been hers. We stopped by and drew water from the well in the courtyard of the present house—the same well that served Lottie and her many guests. As Lottie drank from that well, she must have wished the people of her neighborhood would receive the living water Jesus offers.

A short walk down the narrow cobblestone street—really an alley more than a street—and we came to the intersection at the Monument Street Church. Near the church, an ancient

warlord had built an elaborate gateway monument to honor his parents. The church took its name from that monument.

T.P. Crawford founded and served as pastor of the church throughout his tenure in Tengchow. Lottie quickly found her own ministry in the schools started by other women in the mission. Martha Crawford, Edmonia Moon, and Sallie Holmes (whose husband had been murdered by bandits outside the city in 1862) taught in schools for girls. An obelisk in front of the church recognizes and commends the work of Lottie Moon. No mention is made of T.P. Crawford himself, who had a reputation among both his missionary colleagues and Chinese Christians for dissension and a critical, domineering spirit.

I was not prepared for the emotional experience of worship on Sunday morning in the Monument Street Church. Reliving missions history was overwhelming enough. But the service itself—in an auditorium packed with Chinese Christians fervently worshiping Jesus Christ—brought tears to my eyes. After being closed for many years, the church had only reopened in 1988. Pastor Qin Jai Ye said the church had only twenty members then. Now it has more than 400. The church baptized sixty new believers the year before our visit. In 1994 the church built another worship center across town where more than 100 people gather each Sunday.

The reverence of the worship service communicated that

'We were thrilled to visit the churches and meet with Christians throughout our journey, but we could not escape the awareness of the multitudes around us still untouched by the gospel.'

—*Jerry Rankin*

▶ *'There is
salvation in no one
else; for there is no
other name under
heaven that has
been given among
men, by which we
must be saved.'*

—*Acts 4:12*

this was an experience not to be taken lightly. Those long forbidden to worship publicly, along with new Christians who had only recently discovered the living Savior, now stood together in awe of a mighty God on the throne of grace. God truly inhabits the praises of His people!

The believers sang each hymn with conviction and fervor. The leader paused after each verse to read the words of the next, elaborating briefly on their meaning. Since they don't have all the educational materials and resources we have in our churches, they use the hymns as tools to explain the doctrines and practical expressions of our faith. I started with surprise during this May service when the congregation launched into *It Came Upon the Midnight Clear.* Later someone explained to me it was the same tune but different words from those we know. Nevertheless, it occurred to me how coincidental it was that we would be commemorating Lottie Moon, worshiping in her church, and hearing a song we identify with the Christmas season when we give in her name.

We could not understand the words, but the hour-long sermon by seventy-two-year-old Pastor Qin was obviously powerful. He preached on the Beatitudes taught by Jesus Christ in Matthew 5:10-11. Charlie Wilson, who helps coordinate the work of our Cooperative Services International personnel in China, whispered sketchy excerpts of translation. The pastor spoke of the blessing of being persecuted, but went on

to stress that the key phrase in the passage comes in the words of Jesus in verse 11: "on account of Me."

Persecution comes not for our own righteousness' sake, nor to punish us for evil, but so we can identify with Christ. Persecution is for His sake, that He might be glorified and His kingdom extended. We must never think of ourselves, but of Jesus. Pastor Qin spoke of a stalk of wheat which, when it matures, bends its head of grain lower. The more we mature in Christ, the more humble we become.

Far left: *This monument reminds visitors to the courtyard of Monument Street Church, like Bobbye and Jerry Rankin, of Lottie Moon's legacy.*

Left: *In Monument Street Church, where Lottie Moon ministered in Tengchow, China, Qin Jai Ye brings a message to a congregation of members and visitors.*

Twice during the sermon the pastor broke into beautiful, melodious song to illustrate a point. When he spoke of "hungering and thirsting for righteousness" he tearfully tilted his head and pressed his cheek to his Bible. He told of the brutal persecution of the 1966-76 Cultural Revolution led by the Communist Red Guards, when no one had a Bible. One day he found an old, tattered Bible, and it became very precious to him. How I wish I could have understood the entire message! I sat there not comprehending the words, but feeling my soul being fed. Our tour guide and interpreter had never before stepped inside a church. He later described the experience: "As the people sang and prayed and I listened to the words of the preacher, I felt my spirit was being lifted. It was like a cleansing inside, unlike anything I have experienced before." God's Word is a living fire, a two-edged sword that pierces with conviction to the depths of one's being. Because the Holy Spirit indwells the message of the gospel, it is the power of God unto salvation. How faithful and diligent we

Right: **Members of Monument Street Church fill the aisles for an early-morning prayer service.**

Far right: **Throughout the church, Bibles are open during the worship service. Even today, Bibles in China are a rare and cherished commodity.**

must be to proclaim it and allow it to do its work of grace in the hearts of the lost.

We walked the narrow streets, explored the watergate built long ago as a protection against pirates, and climbed to the Eight Immortals Pavilion, famous throughout China, on a hilltop overlooking the harbor. The pavilion was built over an extended period, beginning in the ninth century, and was a familiar landmark as Lottie sailed in and out of this harbor. The sights and smells of the docks, fish boats, and sampans in the harbor have changed little in the last 120 years. We passed by the beach where Lottie wrote about celebrating Fourth of July picnics with her American colleagues.

Chefoo had become accustomed to foreigners in her day, but here in Tengchow they were resented and despised. Lottie never got used to being called a "foreign devil" whenever she went out. Although heads still turned and children crowded around us wherever we went in modern-day Penglai, we didn't draw the curiosity and attention I would have expected. The Chinese economy is growing rapidly, construction abounds, and joint-venture companies make foreigners a

rather common sight in many places in China today.

In the marketplace, we observed some of the elderly ladies hobbling on tiny feet and were reminded that Lottie spoke out against the practice of footbinding. Lottie struggled with this issue, but in the end enrolled girls who had bound feet in the hope she could reach the parents through the child. Although she worked hard to adapt to Chinese culture, she and her missionary colleagues did not hesitate to confront injustice. In fact, it was unheard of for girls in the area to be educated at all before missionary Sallie Holmes opened her school in 1862. As a schoolteacher, Lottie naturally felt drawn to this method of reaching families with the gospel, and quickly settled into the role. In 1878 she started her own school on North Street and developed an effective witness in the homes of prominent families throughout the city.

In the afternoon we returned to Yantai and met with Tian Li Zhu, the young pastor of the church there. He reported that more than 600 new believers had been baptized the previous year. They counted more than 2,000 members in the Yantai church, but only about 900 could crowd into the two levels of the worship hall and overflow rooms. He was struggling to nurture approximately 100 meeting points throughout the municipality. He asked us to pray especially for young people to be called to serve the growing number of congregations produced by explosive Christian growth.

Most of the pastors in China are quite old and there is a void in leadership, he explained, echoing the words of others we met throughout our journey. Many lay leaders are trying to shoulder the responsibility of the churches, but they lack training and resources. It inspired us to hear the optimism and faith of Pastor Tian, who had been ordained just two years earlier and was ministering so effectively. We gathered around him in a prayer of intercession and encouragement as he faces such a challenging responsibility.

We had only begun to glimpse what God is doing in Shandong Province. As we sensed the growth and vitality of the churches in this part of China, I recalled it was here that a generation of missionaries following Lottie reported a great outpouring of God's Spirit in the late 1920s and early '30s. It came to be known as the Shantung Revival. During my years at seminary I had personally heard missionaries Charles Culpepper and Bertha Smith, who experienced this revival, tell how God moved upon the churches and brought both missionaries and Chinese believers to repentance and miraculous manifestations of faith.

A representative of the local Christian council reported that at least 600,000 registered believers now live in the province; 50,000 of them were baptized in 1994. They count 926 churches and more than 4,000 meeting points or house churches. He knew of forty-one churches started in 1993; that number had

'Conduct yourselves with wisdom toward outsiders, making the most of the opportunity. Let your speech always be with grace, seasoned, as it were, with salt, so that you may know how you should respond to each person.'

—Colossians 4:5-6

> ❧ '...today, despite a Communist government, [Monument Street Church] and many like it affirm that God always preserves a remnant for Himself and that His kingdom will prevail.'
>
> —Jerry Rankin

increased to seventy-nine in 1994. The report sounded like others we receive from all over the world as the number of Baptist churches in countries where our missionaries serve have doubled in just the last six years. More than 2,000 congregations were organized worldwide in 1993 and again in 1994.

I thought of the Monument Street Church, which has been a beacon of light for the gospel for 130 years. The cultural elite of the community failed to squelch its beginning and growth in the nineteenth century. The Boxer Rebellion at the turn of the century and its opposition to anything Western failed to crush its witness for Jesus Christ. The Red Guards, while successful in closing its doors for a brief period during the Cultural Revolution, could not silence the faithful preaching of Jesus Christ and Him crucified. And today, despite a communist government, this church and many like it affirm that God always preserves a remnant for Himself and that His kingdom will prevail.

However, almost 100 million people live in Shandong Province—equal to more than a third of the entire U.S. population. Despite the miraculous survival and growth of the Christian church, fewer than 1 percent of these people have embraced the gospel of Jesus Christ. We were thrilled to visit the churches and meet with Christians throughout our journey, but we could not escape the awareness of the multitudes around us still untouched by the gospel. We prayed that they

Left: **This woman is the granddaughter of one of the six men who helped establish the Huanghsien church. She moved to Tengchow in 1925 to serve as a physician and has been a member of the Monument Street Church since that time.**

Below: **The Rankins pause to refresh themselves with water from the well Lottie used while living at "Little Crossroads."**

Below right: **In 1881, one of Lottie Moon's converts drew a map of the Shantung Mission. Mary Hartwell labeled it, identifying** villages in the North China area where Lottie was working. Lottie then sent it to Henry Tupper so he could report on her efforts there.

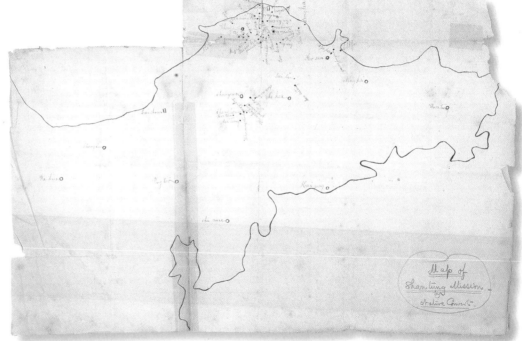

all might come to an awareness of the message of Acts 4:12 emblazoned in big red letters just inside the entrance of the Monument Street Church:

There is salvation in no one else; for there is no other name under heaven that has been given among men, by which we must be saved.

ꬾ 'The primary
role for missionary
women, whether
single or married,
was teaching
school. This suited
Lottie, a trained
and devoted
teacher, just fine for
awhile—until she
discovered the joy
and responsiveness
in village
evangelistic work.'

—Jerry Rankin

ottie had not been in China long before she recognized something was wrong with her sister Edmonia. She refused to acknowledge the hints from veteran missionaries that Edmonia had not adjusted well to China and was suffering increasing stress. Lottie believed her sister's loneliness would be alleviated by her arrival, but Edmonia's problem went deeper than a need for companionship. Instead of growing in her language skills and identification with the Chinese, she had begun to withdraw and demonstrate more frequent evidence of distress and irrational behavior.

The missionaries shared accounts of others who had experienced mental breakdown and nervous exhaustion, and Lottie saw the debilitating physical effects the mission field had on her colleagues. She arranged for Edmonia to have periods of rest, but soon recognized her sister could no longer cope with the challenges of China. Having gone to China

Left: "When I think myself threatened with nervous prostration, I quit work at once and take perfect rest," wrote Lottie Moon in June 1899. Constant overwork and very little hope of being relieved by fresh recruits felled many a missionary in China, including Lottie's sister Edmonia. As symbolized by the two trees shown at left, Edmonia's missions zeal began to wane just as Lottie's began to flourish.

"never to return," Lottie returned to Virginia after only three years in order to bring Edmonia home. She stayed for almost a year and, in her forthright style, began to plant seeds of mission support as she told friends and churches of the lost multitudes of China.

Edmonia never regained enough strength and stamina to return to China with Lottie. Even today, some people for various reasons cannot endure the adjustments and challenges of the mission field. One of the most difficult responsibilities of the Foreign Mission Board staff is to turn down missionary candidates who sense God's call to missions—but who display the likelihood of developing problems once on the field.

The missionary appointment process is not a "screening" procedure. Rather, the board's mission personnel consultants enter into a partnership of discerning God's leadership with those responding to an overseas call. Through many years of experience in sending out more than 12,000 missionaries, the Foreign Mission Board has learned to identify the calling and character traits of those equipped to handle a life of cross-cultural adjustments. Appropriate education, practical experience, spiritual maturity, and interpersonal relationship skills are all essential to effective adjustment and ministry.

In its early years, the board would consider appointing almost anyone in good health and willing to go—as long as funds were available. Sometimes the newly approved

missionaries found themselves on a departing ship soon after being appointed missionaries, with no orientation or additional preparation. Eventually a one-week orientation provided some minimal training for the field. In 1967 the board began a training program of up to sixteen weeks to better equip missionaries for the transition they would face in leaving American culture, encountering a new language, and beginning ministry overseas. Refinement of the program has

the shortened missions careers so common in earlier years.

When Lottie returned to China, she launched a campaign advocating furloughs back home for missionary families. The missionaries of her era missed home and family just as missionaries today do. But homesickness wasn't what Lottie felt justified her request; she believed a periodic respite from the mission field would provide missionaries needed rest, assure longevity, and result in more people being reached with the gospel over a lifetime of witness. Her appeals intensified later as she recognized the value of returning to the United States to share with the churches the need for more laborers and to personally appeal for support. Foreign Mission Board leaders finally agreed, and a furlough policy was later approved. However, it would be 1891, almost twenty years after her initial arrival in China, before Lottie would take her first "official" furlough.[1]

By the time of my missionary appointment in 1970, a four-year term on the field and one-year furlough had become standard. Previously, mission fields were categorized according to hardship, climate, and health conditions. Missionaries assigned to those fields considered most difficult were allowed to return to the United States after three years. In more developed countries, they were expected to serve five years between each furlough.

Today convenient travel options abound, and family needs

*Far left: **At the docks of the seacoast city of Tengchow, workers build huge fishing boats with hand tools much as they did when Lottie lived in China.***

*Above: **A man checks the vigor of his crop in the countryside of Shandong Province, where agriculture continues to provide employment for millions.***

resulted in an eight-week program at the Missionary Learning Center in Rockville, Virginia.

In order to be more sensitive and responsive to those who experience physical and emotional problems today, a professional staff of doctors and counselors ministers to the health needs of missionaries and their families. This has promoted healing and rehabilitation when problems emerge, longer missionary tenure, and more productive service—instead of

James B. Hartwell (right), in Tengchow before Lottie's arrival, was open to the idea of female missionaries. The idea also was beginning to find receptive minds at the Foreign Mission Board under Tupper's leadership in 1872. Reflecting on this potential new role for women, one person said, "This change is in harmony with the Scripture."

are varied. So the Foreign Mission Board allows missionaries to choose furlough options ranging from two to fourteen months, based on terms of service overseas that stretch two to five years. With current furlough policies, health needs receive attention. Opportunities for rest and additional training contribute to long-term effectiveness. And supporting churches know much more about God's work overseas through direct contact with their missionaries.

Another challenge Lottie faced was the lack of a predetermined mission strategy. The board of managers (now called trustees) and corresponding secretary (now president) of the Foreign Mission Board traveled infrequently overseas and had no missionary experience themselves. The distance to China, and the months it took to communicate with the home office, made it impractical for missionaries to depend on guidance from Richmond. On the field, missionaries were left to their own insights and preferences as to the methods they used. For better or worse, the senior missionary on the scene usually set the course and presumed to assert authority over those who arrived later.

T.P. Crawford was such a person. Lottie, forced by policy to join Edmonia in boarding in the Crawford home, not only felt her independence and initiative stifled, but found herself in conflict with established strategies. The primary role for missionary women, whether single or married, was teaching

school. This suited Lottie, a trained and devoted teacher, just fine for awhile—until she discovered the joy and responsiveness in village evangelistic work.

Crawford had founded a church in Tengchow and served as its pastor. But his lack of feeling for Chinese sensitivities, sadly true of many missionaries who followed him, resulted in American-style churches, institutions, and programs being followed. For example, he built a steeple on the church and a second floor on his home, causing these structures to tower over the surrounding community. Chinese neighbors took such offense that he had to use arms to defend himself and the compound from angry mobs.

Joint decision making among the missionaries was expected, but the philosophical conflicts in Tengchow grew so intense that J.B. Hartwell relocated to Chefoo City. Later, when he returned to Tengchow, approval was given to the Foreign Mission Board treasurer back in Richmond to deal with Crawford and Hartwell as two separate mission stations. At one point Crawford appealed to Richmond to exclude women from the business sessions of the mission. Lottie wrote to Tupper predicting that if that policy were adopted, Crawford, the only man remaining in the station, would assume the role of dictator. She offered to resign if such a situation developed.[2]

Later Crawford questioned the authority of the Foreign Mission Board itself. The Landmark controversy was raging in the Southern Baptist Convention, and he gained support for his view that only local churches should send and support missionaries. Most of the North China Mission followed his leadership to withdraw from the Foreign Mission Board and form the Gospel Mission. Lottie remained loyal to the board, but the missionary force was depleted. These tensions became such an administrative burden that Tupper resigned as corresponding secretary of the Foreign Mission Board in 1893. But after Crawford's death, Lottie led an appeal for reconciliation and acceptance of her former colleagues back into the Foreign Mission Board fold.

I find it difficult to comprehend the challenge those early leaders of the Foreign Mission Board must have faced. James B. Taylor led the board from 1846 until 1871, trying to launch the missions efforts of the new denomination with neither resources nor a truly unified base of support. Correspondence with the churches was difficult enough; it was almost impossible with the missionaries far away in China and Africa. Then the Civil War devastated American society. Tupper came into leadership during the Reconstruction years. He faced a constant barrage of controversy at home and schism on the field. I marvel at his wisdom and grace as he advised the missionaries with an attitude of conciliation and support.

Today our Foreign Mission Board staff begins each day with prayer, and I have encouraged a prayer chain throughout the day in our building. As we deal with decisions of international importance and respond to misunderstandings—internal and external—I also sense the thousands of Southern Baptists who must be lifting me and our staff in prayer each day. I am grateful for the counsel of godly people when faced with issues that require the wisdom of Solomon. As I review our history, I find inspiration in these outstanding administrators who laid the foundation and handled similar problems and challenges with far fewer resources.

Missionaries serving together in particular countries still organize themselves as "missions," with the responsibility for developing and coordinating strategies. Over the years the pendulum has swung back and forth between a high degree of autonomy on the field and more administrative authority from the board in Richmond. With missionaries now assigned to more than 130 nations and multiple people groups, it's impossible to have a single worldwide strategy. History and cultures vary considerably from one region to another, as do levels of responsiveness to the gospel and maturity of Baptist work.

The lessons have been painful at times as we continue to develop mission strategy and discover the most effective method of administration and decision making. We continue to recognize that planning must originate on the field. Missionaries involved in implementing the work must have a high level of "ownership" in determining their ministry and meth-

'We are opposed to building foreign chapels, thinking them a great mistake in our part of China. A small humble room with a few plain benches in Chinese style would be proper, and if in time we have converts, they should provide the place of worship.'

—Lottie Moon, July 10, 1886

Right: **Southern Baptist representative Charlie Wilson doubles as a tour guide near Oxner Hospital. Built by Southern Baptists, the hospital was used as a political indoctrination center during the Cultural Revolution.**

Far right: **Rankin kneels beside a drum inside a ward room at Oxner Hospital. The drum is silent now, but the Red Guard played it loudly and often to elevate the devotion of young radicals for Chairman Mao. A picture of the formidable leader hangs above.**

ods of witness. This give and take increases our appreciation for the struggles of those who went before us and, in spite of problems and conflicts, persevered and were used by God.

One example of strategic field initiative was the establishment of medical mission work overseas. While touring Shandong Province we made a brief stop by the Oxner Hospital, where Lottie stayed right before she died. It was built by Southern Baptists between 1907-1909. At times, Southern Baptist medical personnel lived in P'ingtu (now Pingdu) and worked at Oxner. The once-impressive structure was crumbling and awaited demolition when we saw it. Time did not allow us to go to Hwangshien (now Huangxian), where the Foreign Mission Board started its first hospital overseas—the

Warren Memorial Hospital—at the request of the North China Mission. Financed largely by the First Baptist Church of Macon, Georgia, the hospital was built in 1903 with an appropriation of $7,000. Lottie often visited the missionaries in the Hwangshien station and even stayed there to help care for patients when most of the doctors and missionaries had evacuated at the height of the Boxer Rebellion.

Medical missions continues to be a strategic ministry in reaching our world for Christ. In the early years of missionary outreach, medical treatment for the sick, injured, and infirm was practically nonexistent except in developed Western nations. Following the model and admonition of Jesus, we believe providing compassionate care for the sick and needy is

≥▲ 'Estimates of the numbers of Christians in China today range from 35 million to 75 million and more. No one knows for sure how many there are, but we do know the Spirit of God is moving powerfully throughout China.'

—Jerry Rankin

valid in itself. But it also usually opens the door to trust and provides a hearing for the gospel. A hospital was an accepted element of mission strategy when missionaries entered many countries in the past. Today, the expansion of education and technology has brought advanced medical facilities to many areas of the world. Socialized medicine, government clinics, and community health workers now provide alternatives to the one-time monopoly of mission hospitals.

With limited funds and the high cost of providing facilities and modern medical equipment, medical missions today must be evaluated from a different perspective. Baptists overseas have assumed responsibility for many of the mission hospitals. National Christian doctors and nurses have decreased dependence on medical missionaries. The roles for medical missionaries are diversifying through assignments to government medical institutions, community health work, and mobile clinics as well as mission hospitals.

Yet requests for new health-care missionaries continue to greatly exceed the number being appointed. And the Foreign Mission Board continues to support medical ministries on almost every continent. In 1994 our thirty-one Baptist hospitals overseas treated more than 180,000 inpatients and about 2 million outpatients.[3] Each of those patients received a Christian witness. Wherever these hospitals minister, many new churches have sprouted as a result.

Despite their philosophical battles, Lottie Moon and T.P. Crawford agreed on at least one thing: providing subsidies for "native workers" and churches is a mistake. They firmly believed that Baptist work begun on the mission field should be self-supporting and independent of resources from abroad. Although this policy was often compromised, they recognized the potential for maximum growth of work was contingent on its being indigenous. Continuous financial support from abroad, they knew, would create dependency and quench spontaneous expansion of the church.

"We are opposed to building foreign chapels, thinking them a great mistake in our part of China," Lottie wrote in July 1886. "A small humble room with a few plain benches in Chinese style would be proper, and if in time we have converts, they should provide the place of worship."[4] If the Foreign Mission Board had built churches and paid Chinese pastors and evangelists in those early days, as it later did in other parts of the world, we probably would not have seen the explosive growth of the church in China after missionaries had to leave in 1950.

Right: **Not long into her ministry overseas, Lottie began to adopt the Chinese dress. Besides covering, in her estimation, "a multitude of faults," it also helped her relate better to the people. She is shown here with Japanese students during her brief stay in Japan at a time of social unrest in China.**

Far right: **Visitors enter the narrow doorway of the Xi Li He (pronounced she-LIE-huh) church. Attempts to preserve Asian appearance were part of Lottie's strategy to "make friends before we can hope to make converts"—the heart of the board's indigenous principle still being practiced today.**

Today, the Chinese government has adopted this indigenous principle as official policy for Christianity in China. Approved churches affiliate with the Three-Self Patriotic Movement, which expresses the basic tenets of indigenous church growth: self-government, self-support, and self-propagation. The government intends this to prevent interference from abroad, but it also remains essential for the health, growth, and multiplication of the church.

Estimates of the number of Christians in China today range from 35 million to 75 million and more.[5] No one knows for sure how many there are, but we do know the Spirit of God is moving powerfully throughout China. Christian believers numbered approximately 700,000 to 3 million in 1949 when the Communists forced missionaries to leave.[6] The church eventually was driven underground. But in spite of persecution, legal barriers, imprisoned and exiled leadership, and no open places of worship and assembly, the Chinese church experienced one of the greatest growth rates of any country in all of Christian history. This should remind us, as we focus on expanded facilities and beautifully decorated sanctuaries, that the church is built not on external amenities but on faith and sacrifice.

Lottie Moon discovered another important principle that has become a model for subsequent generations of missionaries. She wrote an interesting letter back to her supporters and Baptist newspapers early in her tenure. In it, she advocated the wearing of American dress and maintaining distinct customs and behavior in order not to identify with the pagan culture of China. But whenever she went out she was confronted with the "foreign devil" insult as she tried to mingle with the people. She quickly discovered that when she dressed as they did and began to identify with their lifestyle, she was accepted and received respect. She wrote on March 19, 1887, "I am more and more impressed by the belief that to win these people to God we must first win them to ourselves."[7] Pictures of Lottie in subsequent years always portray her in her traditional Chinese robes. Being only four feet, three inches tall, she easily fit in with the people and lost most vestiges of foreignness among them.

We call this the "incarnational" principle. Missionaries must live their faith in a lifestyle of identification that allows the people who observe them to see the reality of a living Savior. The gospel transcends culture; it is not limited to Western forms of behavior. The Foreign Mission Board spares no effort in providing adequate resources and opportunities to new missionaries for language learning. This initial endeavor on the field is not just the study of vocabulary and grammatical syntax, but the development of communication skills, of learning how people in a different culture think and relate. We encourage missionaries to immerse themselves in the culture and life of the people, living in their kind of houses, eating their kind of food, and building friendships that win a hearing for the gospel.

Lottie found this difficult in the hostile urban environment of Tengchow. It was in the villages that God knitted her life inextricably to the lives of the people of China. And this began to be realized as she discovered P'ingtu.

'...in spite of persecution, legal barriers, imprisoned and exiled leadership, and no open places of worship and assembly, the Chinese church experienced one of the greatest growth rates of any country in all of Christian history. This should remind us...that the church is built not on external amenities but on faith and sacrifice.'

—Jerry Rankin

so'I am more and
more impressed by
the belief that to
win these people to
God we must first
win them to
ourselves.'

—*Lottie Moon, March 19, 1887*

Left: ***Just outside the village of Huanghsien, China, Chinese men usher out another day.***

Back in China after escorting Edmonia home, Lottie became more involved in the itinerant village ministry. She had accompanied her missionary colleague, Sallie Holmes, on some earlier excursions into the country-side. She found the simple village people more curious about spiritual matters—and more responsive to her witness. Now she wanted to pursue the ministry on her own.

With an entourage of laborers bearing her sedan chair and church laymen walking along to provide guidance and protection, she would visit as many as ten or twelve villages on the outskirts of Tengchow. Women and children would gather around her— first out of curiosity, but later with intent interest in hearing her teaching. Sometimes Lottie and her co-workers just launched into their "catechism" in the open. But once they were known, they were invited into homes. Seated on the *kang*—a raised platform, heated underneath, that served as table, bed, and seat of honor in Chinese households—Lottie would talk about

Right and far right: **Red paint obscures the communist slogans that once decorated the exterior and interior of the former Muen (Grace) Baptist Church. Jerry Rankin notes that the Chinese character for "chairman" painted on the building is the same word Chinese Christians use for "Lord." Used as an indoctrination center during the Cultural Revolution, the building now serves as storage for the military, but is scheduled for demolition.**

Jesus to as many as could squeeze into the tiny room.

Accustomed to encountering indifference and hostility in the city, Lottie found excitement and satisfaction in this new work in the countryside. She reflected this in her letters home. After one early trip took her about twenty-five miles from the city, she wrote, "We were to them beloved for our word's sake. Instead of regarding us as foreigners whose influence they were to be jealous, they received us with all the warmer affection because we had come from afar for their sakes, and this feeling they sought to constantly awaken in their heathen acquaintances and friends."[1]

Lottie had discovered what so many missionaries find: Their own foreignness opens doors to friendships and a

hearing that otherwise would be impossible. As I ventured into villages and rural areas of Indonesia, I found a warmth and hospitality because of curiosity and affection for things American. I was able to share my personal discovery of spiritual truths in a way that normally would not have been appropriate within that Muslim society. Everywhere I travel overseas, I find such a reception—whether in China, Africa, or Latin America. When people discover an American has left the relative affluence of home and come to live among them by choice, they readily respect the words he or she shares.

After a rigorous two days on the road with Sallie Holmes, Lottie related in one 1878 letter, "I said to Mrs. Holmes very decidedly at the tenth village that I should do no more mis-

And let us not lose heart in doing good, for in due time we shall reap if we do not grow weary. So then, while we have opportunity, let us do good to all men, and especially to those who are of the household of faith.'

—Galatians 6:9-10

sionary work that day, but no sooner had our chair been set down than the people came crowding about us and it was impossible to keep silence. We have 'the words of eternal life' and we must speak them to the people in spite of all weariness.''[2] What a wonderful testimony of the energizing power that comes from sharing the gospel!

In Lottie's day, it was not considered appropriate for women to be involved in such direct evangelistic work, and Lottie pleaded for men to come and take up this work. But missionary men already on the field struggled to care for the churches, translate materials, and handle administrative matters, so Lottie reasoned that the women had to take up the slack. Remem-bering this renewed in me a sense of guilt I had felt

throughout my years of service in Indonesia.

I was constantly aware that I had come to Indonesia to introduce the people to Jesus Christ. Nevertheless, the best intentions and most diligent efforts to put evangelism first often got sabotaged by the scope of mission responsibilities. Meeting family needs, preparing Bible studies and sermons in a difficult language, coping with a barrage of government red tape and registrations that constantly had to be renewed—all these greatly diminished the opportunity to mingle with neighbors and people on the streets or in the marketplace.

Lottie grew frustrated with the time-consuming task of teaching and administering her school, as well as the slow pace of mission outreach such an indirect approach entailed. In

Right: **This Chinese couple own what was once home to Lottie Moon in P'ingtu City. They are seated on a** kang, *a* **platform made of stone. Lottie spent much of her time at home on her** kang *as it was the only heat source. It was warmed by air from the fireplace.**

1879, Henry Tupper of the Foreign Mission Board had endorsed pioneer evangelistic work by missionary women despite the reservations and objections of some on the field. After returning from one of her rural survey trips, Lottie reported the exhilaration and encouragement she had found. "I was much delighted with the wide-open door for woman's work," she wrote. "I have seen nothing comparable to it in my whole missionary experience. Such eager drinking-in of the truth, such teachableness, I have never seen before."[3] She turned over her school to others and began to give herself fully to the village work, eventually centering her outreach in the town of Pingdu. She felt so strongly led in this witness that she

later threatened to resign in 1885 when the Foreign Mission Board seemed less supportive of women in direct evangelism.[4]

From Yantai, it took us more than three hours to reach Pingdu, traveling on a modern highway. Although Lottie traveled directly from Tengchow, it took her days of rigorous travel in a *shentze*, spending the nights in filthy communal inns along the way. She went so readily because she found an eager response to the gospel. Because of her dedication, churches quickly formed after new believers were baptized. She would return to her house at Little Crossroads in Tengchow for a month of rest and recuperation in the summer, then plunge back into the demanding pace of village work for the remainder of the year.

Left: **Cartersville Baptist Church member Dean Milazzo displays a tray of cookies made from Lottie's recipe for "plain tea cake." The cookies helped Lottie gain the trust of Chinese children as well as a new name: "The Cookie Lady."**

Right: **Lottie's primitive oven, where she first baked her popular cookies, also heated the kang on the other side of the wall.**

❧ 'Lottie had discovered what so many missionaries find: Their own foreignness opens doors to friendship and a hearing that otherwise would be impossible.'

—Jerry Rankin

When we arrived in Pingdu, now a bustling prefecture capital city, our first stop was the former P'ingtu City Church. Construction began on it in 1902, and the building was dedicated in 1905, soon after Lottie returned to China for her final term of service. I could only imagine the gratification she must have felt to see this visible testimony to her efforts begun twenty years earlier.

The large deteriorating structure, soon to be demolished to make way for urban growth, had become part of a military compound. The Japanese closed the church December 7, 1941 (the same day Pearl Harbor was attacked), when they took over the city. The communist takeover of China followed

World War II, and the building was used until recently as an indoctrination center. A big red star marks the entrance and fading slogans of the revolution still adorn the walls. The faint outline of huge Chinese characters read, "Ten thousand years Chairman Mao will live," or as commonly translated, "Long live Chairman Mao." Those words rallied the communist revolutionaries who drove the Nationalist government into exile in Taiwan (Formosa) in 1949. Later they inspired the fervent Red Guards, who tore Chinese society apart all over again beginning in 1966. Interestingly, someone on our trip explained that the character for "chairman" is the same word Chinese Christians use for "Lord."

'I fervently pray that the people of China will come to know the living Lord, the One who also died, but rose again and lives as King of kings and Lord of lords.'

—*Jerry Rankin*

Earlier we had visited Tiananmen Square in Beijing and observed the imposing government buildings of the People's Republic of China. Occupying a prominent location on the square is the mausoleum where thousands still file by daily to gaze on the embalmed body of Mao Zedong, leader of the Chinese Communist revolution. Clearly, the people of China know that their venerated leader is dead. His ideology now struggles for survival. I fervently pray that the people of China will come to know the living Lord, the One who also died, but rose again and lives as King of kings and Lord of lords.

Back in Pingdu, we drove to the new location of the church. The government had allowed it to occupy the meeting hall of a religious association that no longer used it. Quickly the congregation overflowed the space. A renovation project expanded the building, and a new pulpit was being constructed while we were there. We rejoiced in the Baptist roots of this congregation—seen in a baptistery for immersion which was under construction. Mr. Liu, an elder of the church, gave us a gracious welcome and spoke of the growth and optimism of the Christians in their freedom to worship. He accepted a gift of newly published study Bibles for two seminary students from Pingdu who assist in the care of the church.

Later, we were eager to grab a quick lunch and see the house where Lottie lived in Pingdu. However, as we had already discovered, no "quick lunch" exists for visitors to China.

The multiple-course meal laid before us had to be consumed slowly and deliberately, as we concentrated on maneuvering each morsel between the pinched tips of chopsticks and into our mouths. After asking our host to identify what turned out to be sea worms, blanched duck legs, and other delicacies, we stopped inquiring about food we didn't recognize.

We made our way through the narrow alleyways of an older section of the city, then turned through an arched gateway into a small compound. There we were received by an elderly couple who had been alerted to our arrival. With all the alleys and nearly identical tile-roofed houses in the neighborhood, I asked how our guide knew this was actually Lottie Moon's house.

Hou Xi Wu of the Pingdu Tourist Development bureau told us he was contacted by the Woman's Missionary Union when they were taking tours to "Lottie Moon's China" in 1987 and 1988 on the occasion of the WMU centennial. He had been asked to try to locate this house. He did extensive research, and visited more than fifty families living in this section of town, which dated from the nineteenth century. But he just about gave up hope of finding anyone who could connect a house with the famous missionary.

Then one day he went into a barbershop. There he heard an elderly man mention that his grandfather had bought the house he was living in from a man who once had leased it to

an American missionary. Mr. Hou asked the elderly man if he knew the name of that missionary. He replied that he wasn't certain, but thought it was something like "La Di Mu." Mr. Hou followed him home and found a house that matched the photos and descriptions he had been given.

Lottie spent her most fulfilling years in this house in the heart of the city. Still in good condition, the three-room home is built in traditional Chinese style with the center room serving as an entrance hallway that allows access out the front and the back. In one corner of this room, just inside the front door, sits a small brick oven used for cooking and heat. To one side is a living area, where the family takes its meals. On the other side of the hallway is the bedroom where Lottie's chest of drawers still rests. On the wall closest to the front is the raised brick platform called the *kang*. A conduit that comes through the wall from the oven in the grand hallway keeps the *kang* warm. Here people sit and visit socially during the day. At night a bedroll is laid out for sleeping. It hardly seems comfortable, but Lottie spoke lovingly of the time she spent on the *kang*, conversing with her eager audience about Jesus and His love.

In this same oven, Lottie made her first batch of sugar cookies, which she used as an evangelistic tool with the children. Her "tea cake" recipe, which originated in Virginia, has survived to this day, and is found both in China and in America. People still love to serve "Lottie Moon" cookies as refresh-

ments for fellowships. Instead of the "foreign devil woman" she had been called earlier in Tengchow, she became known in other Chinese cities as the "cookie lady." She earned a hearing for sharing the Bread of Life. Children were especially responsive to her, gathering in the courtyard outside her home and around her *kang* when invited inside. Today the children of the area still become intrigued by foreign visitors. Every time our caravan paused at a site, word quickly spread that the Westerners had arrived. Within minutes a sea of people surrounded us. Adults approached somewhat cautiously, but the children ran right up to talk. It's easy to see why Lottie had no trouble drawing a crowd of women and children to hear her songs and stories about Jesus.

Lottie didn't limit her witness to Pingdu, but continued to tour the surrounding villages. Mr. Hou said he had discovered thirty-five churches in the Pingdu District that rose from the foundation she laid and the ministry of missionaries who followed her. As touching as worship had been at the Monument Street Church in Penglai the day before, we were in for our most meaningful experience as we followed a little dirt road on a circuit of villages just outside the city.

Huanghsien village was where Lottie's first converts were baptized. No church building exists there today, but a strong group of believers still meets in the home of a grandson of one of the original members of the church. Minutes after we

In the late 1800s, Lottie turned over her school to others, giving herself fully to village work. She centered her efforts out of Pingdu, often riding in a **shentze** *(left), her rigorous days punctuated by nights in filthy communal inns along the way.*

> *'Revolutions may come and go. The church may be closed and society regimented. But the faith of those believers has never wavered as they have walked with their Lord and quietly, perhaps secretly, celebrated their confidence in an eternal home.'*
>
> —*Jerry Rankin*

stopped there, a large group of people gathered, many of them third- and fourth-generation Christians who have remained faithful for these many years. Lottie first mentioned this community in a letter to Dr. Tupper in August 1888: "The people . . . are urgent to have me live among them. They say that they must have a teacher, that many of them are determined to be Christians, and no amount of obloquy [censure] can keep them back."[5] Lottie went, the people were saved, and the first six believers were baptized by C.W. Pruitt, a missionary colleague.

Leaning against a wall in the municipal building is a marble tablet with a detailed history of the church and the first believers. It tells of Lottie Moon coming to witness and encourage the new Christians, and her subsequent support in the early years. It also mentions William H. Sears, who took up responsibility for missionary work in the Pingdu area in later years. This note brought an interesting personal connection into perspective. Sears was the grandfather of Stockwell Sears, one of the three ex-China missionaries who opened Southern Baptist work in Indonesia in 1951. Stockwell and his wife, Darlyne, started Baptist work in Surabaya, the capital of East Java, where I was later assigned as a church planter. They eventually transferred to Singapore and Malaysia, where we were privileged to relate to them prior to their retirement.

Many other missionaries, appointed to China but forced to leave when the country came under communist control, led in

A young deacon works in a tofu factory owned by the church in Xi Li He, China. Proceeds from tofu sales help underwrite the church's work. Lottie helped establish this church before the turn of the century.

> &❧ 'While the great metropolitan areas of the world must be reached with the gospel—and we are making every effort to do so today with urban evangelism strategies —invariably the initial response is in the village. The simple lifestyle and lack of sophistication found there allow people to be more open to the gospel.'
>
> —Jerry Rankin

the expansion of Southern Baptist missions as they dispersed to the Philippines, Thailand, Singapore, Malaysia, Indonesia, Taiwan, Korea, and Hong Kong. Some had already retired when we arrived in 1971. But we will be forever indebted to the godly servant spirit and exemplary commitment of colleagues such as Wilma Weeks, Catherine Walker, Everley Hayes, Evelyn Schwartz, and others who came from China and became our mentors. They didn't see the closure of China as defeat, but as the providence of God using political circumstances to give Southern Baptists a larger global vision and extend His kingdom even further.

Literacy was not a high priority in rural China before the introduction of the gospel. When Lottie left to return to the city, she had to leave the Scripture in the hands of a Confucian scholar named Li Show Ting, who could read portions of it to those already converted. At first the scholar was scornful, but the Word of God is sharper than any two-edged sword, able to separate man from his sinful past and put him on a path toward God. After serious study of the Bible, Li Show Ting came to faith in Christ and went on to become a prominent evangelist. He was a forerunner of the famous Shantung Revi-

val, and supposedly baptized more than 10,000 converts during his ministry. A monument to his memory and leadership was recently discovered in the village.

As we disembarked from the bus at this site, an elderly man made his way through the crowd gathered around us. He was Li Show Ting's grandnephew. Now quite elderly himself, he proudly declared he has six grown sons—all of whom are Christians. That is a phenomenal fact in this era when most Chinese families are allowed only one child, and when the national ideology is supposed to have eliminated religious beliefs over the last 45 years.

The story of Li Show Ting illustrates the desire of every missionary: to multiply oneself through local believers who in turn expand the witness of the gospel far beyond what one person could do. I'll always remember when I first heard about Bold Mission Thrust in 1976. Southern Baptists had adopted a vision of reaching every person in the world with the gospel by the end of the century. At that time I was the only missionary in an

Far left: Visitors from the United States tour the interior of the Fourth P'ingtu Church in the Xi Li He area.

Left: Church members greet the visitors just outside the building. The church, said to be the oldest church building in the area, was built almost 100 years ago and has changed little since Lottie Moon worshiped there.

area with more than 5 million people on the eastern tip of Java. Never in a lifetime of diligent preaching and witnessing could I personally touch that many people. But as a few were touched and responded to the gospel, churches were started. I would return to encourage and disciple these infant congregations, train leaders, and find that they already were sharing the gospel with neighboring communities and villages. Such leaders are the ones who build God's kingdom around the world upon the foundation laid by missionaries who came introducing people to the Savior.

This brings into focus what has become a priority: training local leaders. Foreign Mission Board workers labor in 156 Bible schools and seminaries around the world as well as more than

900 programs of Theological Education by Extension. These schools and programs enrolled more than 30,000 students in 1994.[6] That number must vastly increase to meet the leadership needs of the explosive church growth taking place today. Christian leaders in China are asking us to pray for church members to be called into the ministry. Most of the Chinese pastors are in their seventies and eighties, and the need for a new generation of leaders grows critical.

God continues to give gifts to His church. I always sought to plant churches with the confidence God would raise up the leaders needed by each congregation, anointing them with spiritual gifts for the completion of the body. We saw this affirmed in China as lay leaders and "Bible women" nurtured

'I commented at one of the churches we visited that we had come to walk in the steps of a missionary of a former era. But we had discovered we were walking in the steps of Chinese Christians who continue the journey of faith....'

—Jerry Rankin

village churches and continued the evangelistic impetus begun by Lottie Moon and others. I commented at one of the churches we visited that we had come to walk in the steps of a missionary of a former era. But we had discovered we were walking in the steps of Chinese Christians who continue the journey of faith and are being used of God to exalt Jesus Christ in an expanding witness.

We had come to Huanghsien, arriving about sunset, after passing through Qi Li He village. "Li" is the common Chinese measure of distance; it equals about half a kilometer or a third of a mile. Qi Li He means "the brook seven li from the city." There we found an L-shaped church built in 1898.

When we came to Qi Li He, people came out of nearby houses and cautiously drifted into the courtyard of the church. Among the first to arrive were several elderly ladies hobbling on canes, their faces deeply wrinkled with age. One told of her grandfather working as an evangelist with Li Show Ting. They all had a glow of serenity that indicated they knew from experience the faithfulness and abiding peace only their Savior could provide.

In this remote village, I felt we touched the heart of Christianity in China. Revolutions may come and go. The church may be closed and society regimented. But the faith of these believers has never wavered as they have walked with their Lord and quietly, perhaps secretly, celebrated their con-

fidence in an eternal home.

As we were leaving, we asked the group if they would sing for us. They joyously launched into all six verses of *Jesus Loves Me*. This is known as "the Lottie Moon hymn" in China. In fact, the tune name in our hymnals in America is *China*. She taught it to the children and sang it throughout her lifetime. We wiped away tears as we listened to the familiar melody. Our spirits united with these simple village folk in a remote location half a world away from America. Spontaneously our group sang the familiar hymn in English, then we sang it all together once again before joining in prayer.

The language and appearance of the people may have been different, but I could have closed my eyes and beheld a similar scene in Indonesia, the Philippines, India—in any number of locations I have traveled to on the mission fields. It reminded me that while locations vary, basic missionary principles remain the same. Lottie had followed one of those principles by simply going where the people are responding. It is a principle that continues to be true today.

While the great metropolitan areas of the world must be reached with the gospel—and we are making every effort to do so today with urban evangelism strategies—invariably the initial response is in the village. The simple lifestyle and lack of sophistication found there allow people to be more open to the gospel. And the close-knit social structure of rural people often

Rankin examines a stone tablet relating the early history of the church in Shaling. The original church building fell into disrepair and collapsed, but services continue to be held in the home of a fourth-generation believer.

results in a simultaneous group response—in contrast to the slow, prolonged individual ministry that usually characterizes work in the city.

In China today, a significant number of church buildings have reopened in the cities. They overflow with worshipers each Sunday. But 80 percent of China's people still live in the villages. It is here that believers have kept the faith firmly through persecution and the currents of political change. And it is in the villages, among the rural people of China, where the gospel continues to spread in a rising tide unprecedented in recent Christian history.

'Lottie had been tethered by a lifeline that sustained her and provided for many of her needs. The society in Cartersville had stood, 12,000 miles away, at the other end of the rope.'

—Jerry Rankin

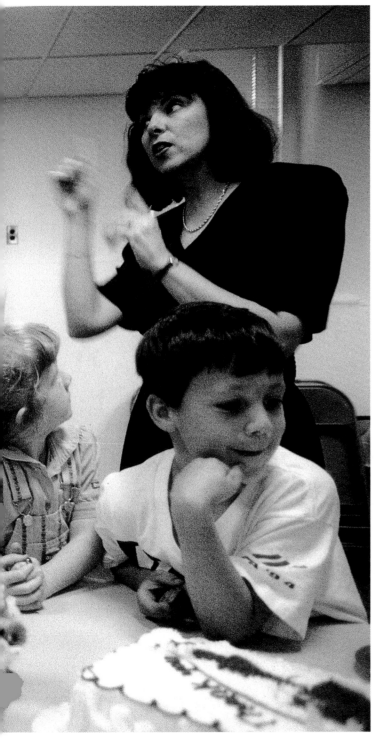

Left: *Much of Lottie Moon's energy was focused on children's education—both stateside and overseas. Jerry Rankin and Dellanna O'Brien chat with a Girls in Action leader and her GAs at First Baptist Church in Cartersville, Georgia.*

Cartersville Baptist Church was neither large enough nor centrally located for a community celebration befitting an honored guest. So the Presbyterians graciously agreed to host the homecoming service for this renowned personage on a warm spring night in May of 1892.

Lottie Moon, on her first missionary furlough, had returned to Cartersville to report on her work in China and thank the people for their support. As she walked to the platform, a breeze from the open windows blew across the people who had crowded into the church to hear this ambassador for Christ.

She looked out on the congregation and saw the faces of those who had prayed for and financially supported her ministry. A fellow teacher here, a former pupil there, an aged deacon on the aisle. Many more, too young to remember her before she went to China, also listened. They all waited expectantly to hear this woman, who had left their community al-

Mary Eliza Shaw, member of the Cartersville church, holds two "mite boxes" her mother used to collect money for Lottie Moon's missionary work.

most twenty years before, share a lifetime of experiences. They weren't disappointed. As she spoke that night and met with groups and individuals over the next few days, Lottie told them of the wonders of China and what God was doing there.

This reunion was especially gratifying to Lottie and her friends in Georgia, because the Woman's Missionary Society there had organized to support her even before she left on her first overseas journey. Minutes of that body's first meeting on August 17, 1873, confirm it as the oldest organization formed in Georgia to support foreign mission work. In an age before

the Cooperative Program and coordinated support for our denominational missions programs, the close connection between missionary and church was essential. Since the women of Virginia had pledged to support Edmonia Moon the year before, the women of Georgia were asked to provide Lottie's support.

They gathered that first night in 1873 a few miles from Cartersville in what was then called the Gilreath House. Anxious to support Lottie and the North China Mission, but also anxious not to do anything to jeopardize the tithe, the women created guidelines that called on members to give sacrificially. "In raising funds," the third article of their constitution reads, "there shall be no interference with the regular missionary contributions of the Church, but our reliance shall be upon mission boxes in our homes into which we pledge ourselves upon becoming members to deposit at least two cents a week upon the first day of every week, this day being preferable as a scriptural injunction."[1] Soon, these mission or "mite" boxes appeared on kitchen windowsills, night stands, and dressing tables in houses all over Cartersville. The ladies had mobilized for support and ministry.

As Lottie rose to speak on her return visit, she had a message for this special group. She turned to the ladies of the Woman's Missionary Society and said, "Right noble have you held the rope." The ladies, in turn, stood and said, "Right noble have you gone into the well."[2] This was a reference to the words of William Carey, the humble English cobbler who ignited the modern evangelical missionary movement when he went to India in 1792. He had said to his group of supporters, "I will go down into the well, if you will hold the rope."[3] For twenty years Lottie had been tethered by a lifeline that sustained her and provided for many of her needs. The society in Cartersville had stood, 7,000 miles away, at the other end of the rope.

One hundred and three years later—almost to the day—Dellanna O'Brien and I stood in First Baptist Church of Cartersville. We thanked the people there for that same faithful support for missions which has continued over the years. We went there to pay tribute to Lottie Moon and the church in which she had responded to the call to missions. As executive director of the Woman's Missionary Union of the Southern Baptist Convention, Dr. O'Brien reflected on the strength of this national organization. It emerged to provide missions education and support, thanks to the local example of the women in Cartersville and other towns many years before. In a dinner with the WMU members at First Baptist prior to the service, she recounted the history of Lottie's missionary career, and later presented a plaque of appreciation to the Cartersville church for its support.

"We all carry Lottie Moon in our hearts. She has become for us what it takes to take God's Word around the world," said Dr. O'Brien, acknowledging the influence and tradition born through the ministry of this Cartersville schoolteacher.

We realized that, even as we celebrated the life and ministry of Lottie Moon, we were really celebrating the role of a local church in fulfilling its missions task. Missionaries come from local churches. It is the local church that gives to support missionaries through the Foreign Mission Board and sustain missionaries through prayer. How appropriate it is for missionaries, as Lottie did in 1892, to return and report to the church the great things God has done through their overseas ministry.

That night we also heard the testimony of Kim Dickey, who had spent two terms with the Foreign Mission Board's International Service Corps as a teacher in China, and was preparing to return. We identified with those who heard Lottie Moon that evening a century ago as Kim told of lives being touched by the gospel in China today.

We enjoyed visiting with the women of the WMU and celebrating the 150th anniversary of the Home and Foreign Mission boards with a birthday cake prepared by the children in Royal Ambassadors, Girls in Action, and Mission Friends. And we recalled Lottie Moon's influence in bringing about the formation of this mighty force for missions among the women of the Southern Baptist Convention. Organized as an auxiliary to the convention in a simultaneous meeting in Richmond in

'We realized that, even as we celebrated the life and ministry of Lottie Moon, we were really celebrating the role of a local church in fulfilling its missions task. Missionaries come from local churches. It is the local church that gives to support missionaries through the Foreign Mission Board and sustain missionaries through prayer.'

—Jerry Rankin

Right: O'Brien listens to the testimony of a director of missions at First Baptist Church, Cartersville, Georgia. In 1995 Southern Baptists from dozens of locales attended the church's tribute to Lottie Moon—one of its more prominent members.

Far right: Kim Dickey, a Southern Baptist now serving in China, shares about life and work on the historic mission field today during the tribute.

1888, the Woman's Missionary Union has grown to more than a million members in local churches. Generating missions support, cultivating missions awareness, and educating successive generations of boys and girls in this primary task of the church, WMU has helped Southern Baptists become the largest career missionary-sending denomination among American Protestants.[4] Even as other missions agencies struggle for support and decline in personnel, the Home and

Foreign Mission boards celebrate record appointments and continue to reach the lost, because of the faithful partnership of this auxiliary organization.

Lottie Moon was a crusader, and she minced no words in her correspondence with Dr. Tupper and the Foreign Mission Board. These letters found their way into the hands of women's missionary societies, and thundered from the pages of state Baptist papers and the *Foreign Mission Journal.* She constantly appealed for additional support that laborers might be sent to the field. These appeals actually grew out of her plea for a furlough. After the unfortunate experience with Edmonia, other colleagues on the field had to return to the United States from exhaustion and physical breakdowns. Lottie saw many missionaries succumb to an early grave after a few years because of the difficult conditions under which they labored.

Dr. Tupper agreed to the principle of a furlough every ten years. Lottie, however, hesitated to leave the field until someone could take her place. Tupper fully supported her return home for a time of respite and speaking in the churches. But the mission board, suffering from debt, couldn't afford to send new missionaries.

In 1886, Lottie wrote of the need for more men and women: "Immense fields lie untoucht (sic) for want of laborers to occupy them."[5] As new missionaries failed to appear, she found herself one of the few missionaries in the North China Mission. And she recognized the symptoms of fatigue and potential health problems in herself.

"Here I am working alone in a city of many thousand inhabitants with numberless villages," she reported. "How many can I reach without help?"[6] It seemed to her a great embarrassment that the churches weren't sending a steady flow of workers to this needy harvest field. She had written in 1878 to Dr. Tupper, "It is odd that the million (or is it a million?)

'Generating missions support, cultivating missions awareness, and educating successive generations of boys and girls in this primary task of the church, WMU has helped Southern Baptists become the largest career missionary-sending denomination among American Protestants.'

—Jerry Rankin

Right: O'Brien and Rankin pose with WMU members of First Baptist Church, Cartersville.

Far right: WMU members gather outside the church in 1903.

Baptists of the South can only furnish three men for China! Odd that with five hundred Baptist preachers in the state of Virginia, we must rely on a Presbyterian minister to fill a Baptist pulpit" in China.[7]

We still get letters like that from our missionaries. More than 700 urgent requests for additional workers came from missions throughout the world last year. They came from Africa and Latin America, where a great harvest cries out for laborers to encourage the churches, train pastors and evangelists, disciple new believers, and proclaim the gospel to a spiritually hungry and responsive population. They came from Asia, where missionaries are overwhelmed by the masses.

While serving in Indonesia, we once calculated that our Baptist mission had one missionary unit for every 6.8 million people. I recall visiting our personnel in Bangladesh, a country the size of Arkansas with 110 million people. At a time of unprecedented church growth there, health problems had depleted the mission to only two couples, who were pleading for reinforcements. New strategies have created opportunities for touching unreached people groups with the gospel—peoples who have been isolated culturally and geographically over the years and deprived of an opportunity to hear of Jesus Christ. But the requests for someone to go to the Makuwe, the Chechens, the Luri, and many other groups remain unfilled. Record numbers of missionaries are being appointed, but in the best

year, no more than 40 percent of the requests will be filled.

Lottie resorted to shaming the churches of the convention for their lack of response to the needs and opportunities in China. She spoke of the Chinese men who would eavesdrop on her teaching of women and girls in the villages, and how ða 'Oh, that my words could be as a trumpet call stirring the hearts of my brethren and sisters to pray, to labor, to give thanks, to give themselves to the people.'

—*Lottie Moon*

unfortunate it was that no Baptist men were interested in coming to preach the gospel. Lottie was concerned that a lack of male workers forced her to have to teach men. After a while, she was reconciled to this necessity, but sensitive that reports of it back home would not be well received. As she pressed forward with the country work, she said, "How inadequate the force! Here is a province of thirty million souls and Southern Baptists can only send one man and three women to tell them the story of redeeming love. Oh, that my words

could be as a trumpet call stirring the hearts of my brethren and sisters to pray, to labor, to give thanks, to give themselves to the people."[8] She even accused Baptists of apparently adopting a "new theology" since they seemed to have a strange indifference to missions.

We are so grateful for the strong support of Southern Baptists today who undergird the work of more than 4,000 missionaries in more than 130 countries. But I often find myself grieved by the many churches that seem to lack a vision for fulfilling the Great Commission. Many seem to draw a circle

On August 17, 1873, some women of the Cartersville Baptist Church (now First Baptist) met in this house and formed a Woman's Missionary Society to aid a young teacher from the community going to China as a missionary—Lottie Moon.

around their community and identify that as their mission, instead of recognizing a responsibility for reaching the whole world. Many spend excessive resources on their own facilities and activities, however worthy they may be, at the expense of support for missions. Yet those who keep the world before their people and encourage support for missions are invariably those being used effectively by God in local ministry as well.

During seminary, I was deeply convicted that a call to ministry and service in surrender to God was a call without geographic restrictions. If a fellow student had not even considered the possibility of missionary service, I often would question the reality of a divine call in his life. I would readily agree with Lottie that a lack of interest in and support of missions must represent a "new theology." It certainly does not come from the heart of God and the teaching of His Word, which has given us a mandate to "Go into all the world and make disciples of all nations."

In 1887, Lottie heard that Methodist women devoted the week before Christmas for prayer and self-denial. She began to advocate this among Baptists. Writing in the *Foreign Mission Journal*, she asked, "Need it be said why the week before Christmas is chosen? Is not the festive season, when families and friends exchange gifts in memory of The Gift laid on the altar of the world for the redemption of the human race, the most appropriate time to consecrate a portion from abounding riches and scant poverty to send forth the good tidings of great joy into all the earth?"[9]

The women in Cartersville already had been collecting their gifts at Christmastime, but it was an idea that captivated the hearts and commitment of Baptist women across the convention. Still unable to take her furlough, Lottie pleaded with the women to raise money to send two women to take her place. Representatives from the various state mission societies and ladies' organizations gathered during the Southern Baptist Convention meeting in Richmond in 1888 and officially organized the Woman's Missionary Union. They were not welcomed in the convention itself; in fact, a delegation from the convention was sent to their meeting to find out what they were up to!

So strong burned their devotion to missions and the support of missionaries, however, that these women were undeterred by critics and those who belittled their efforts. Dr. Tupper met with the WMU Executive Committee in fall 1888 and challenged them to undertake the Christmas offering suggested by Lottie Moon. They took up the challenge and set a goal of $2,000. Within months—and less than a year after Lottie Moon's call to action—the women had raised more than $3,300 to send not two but three new missionaries to China. By 1891 these workers had arrived on the field, learned the language, and assumed responsibilities sufficiently for Lottie to take her long-awaited furlough.

Lottie had strongly advocated the organization of the women of the convention, but she urged that their purpose should remain in focus. "In seeking organization we do not need to adopt plans or methods unsuitable to the view or repugnant to the tastes of our brethren," she wrote. "What we want is not power, but simply combination in order to elicit the largest possible giving. Power of [missionary] appointment and disbursing of funds should be left, as heretofore, in the hands of the Foreign Mission Board. Separate organization is undesirable, and would do harm, but organization in subordination to the Board is the imperative need of the hour."[10]

Thus was forged a partnership that has brought glory to God and served His kingdom. It has enabled Southern Baptists to touch the whole world with the gospel. The Southern Baptist Convention was formed in 1845 for the purpose of doing missions. The Home and Foreign Mission boards also were organized, but it is the Woman's Missionary Union that has acted as the missions conscience of the convention by keeping the responsibility of reaching a lost world before the local churches. The majority of our missionaries have been influenced by the missions education organizations in our churches to sense God's call. In every appointment service, new missionaries testify that a mission study in WMU or the impact of Girls in Action was the most significant influence God used to

impress upon them that personal call to missions.

The idea of a special offering of self-denial for missions at Christmastime caught on and gained momentum. In 1918, six years after Lottie Moon's death, Annie Armstrong, the retired executive director of Woman's Missionary Union, suggested that this annual offering for foreign missions be named for Lottie Moon. Lottie's encouragement and persuasion had resulted in the offering being initiated—and her life epitomized the sacrificial spirit and faithful service for which the offering was given.

Since 1888 the women of WMU have faithfully held the ropes in prayer support, missions education, and financial support for missionaries joining the journey in obedience to God's call. In times of debt, when the work of the Foreign Mission Board was paralyzed, new missionaries could not be sent for lack of support, and others could not take a much-needed furlough due to lack of funds for travel, the WMU mobilized the support, collected their mite boxes, and sacrificed from meager resources to keep the good news of Jesus flowing to the ends of the earth.

This commitment expanded beyond the women in the churches as more and more church members desired to support the cause of missions. After World War II, new waves of Southern Baptist missionaries were appointed to minister to the hurt and devastated world. In 1956 the Christmas offering became denominationwide. In just over 100 years, Southern Baptists have given more than $1.5 billion dollars to the Foreign Mission Board through the Lottie Moon Christmas Offering for Foreign Missions.[12]

The offering continues to be received during the Christmas season in celebration of God's gift to a lost world. It now provides nearly half of the Foreign Mission Board's annual income. One hundred percent of the offering goes to the overseas portion of the budget, primarily for use in missionary support, just as it did in 1888. There was a time when the offering provided for extra capital needs in building churches and institutions overseas. But now, except for a small percentage, it pays for the ever-increasing ministry and operating expenses of a growing missionary force. As we move toward the twenty-first century and face unprecedented opportunities overseas, Southern Baptists are being challenged to give $100 million a year through the Lottie Moon offering—lest appointments begin to be restricted and doors for reaching the lost remain closed.

I think of Dr. Tupper's struggle to keep a small group of missionaries on the field, and the debt that hounded the Foreign Mission Board through the early years of this century. I praise God for the Cooperative Program that came into existence in 1925 as an inspired method of supporting denominational ministries. My earlier predecessors had to rely on agents in the field, who not only had to make the case for foreign missions to the local church, but also had to compete with other organizations for an uncertain portion of the church's receipts. Today, I visit hundreds of churches across our land every year—not to raise funds, but to share what God is doing and to thank them for their faithful support.

I rejoice in the faithful support of the Woman's Missionary Union that helps the spirit of Lottie Moon to live on in missions giving. That cooperative spirit has helped bring Christ to the nations, and it has kept the Southern Baptist missionary effort from becoming bogged down again by indebtedness.

As Dellanna O'Brien and I returned to Cartersville that memorable night in May, we recognized that times have changed, as have many circumstances that affect denominational life. However, some things remain constant. People in China, and all around the world, still need Jesus. Missionaries continue to struggle under their load and plead for reinforcements to join them in answering the call. The Cooperative Program and the Lottie Moon Christmas Offering continue to support the sending of missionaries and reaching our world. And the Woman's Missionary Union continues a journey of faith and sacrifice to serve the cause of missions. ❧

Members of Crewe (Virginia) Baptist Church installed a stained-glass window to memorialize the missions heroine and to extend Christ's command to "Go ye therefore and teach all nations."

GO YE THEREFORE AND TEACH ALL NATIONS

MISS LOTTIE MOON
OUR BELOVED MISSIONARY
BORN DEC 12 1840 – DIED DEC 24 1912.

A s our tour of China came to a close, I felt compelled to read once more through the sheaf of Lottie's letters retrieved from the Foreign Mission Board archives. Her reflections and testimonies took on new meaning for me after I had walked in the villages and cities where she walked.

Although she spent much of her final years in P'ingtu, the house at Little Crossroads in Tengchow became her haven of rest as she caught up on correspondence and reading in the hot summer months. The overhang of the tiled roof created a veranda where she received guests and provided "orientation" for the stream of new missionaries that began to come to the field.

Lottie cherished these times of relaxation when age began to sap her strength. But she refused to diminish her rigorous schedule. "I reach home thanking God for its peace and quiet, rejoicing in the privilege of the past day's work," she wrote a

'I reach home thanking God for its peace and quiet, rejoicing in the privilege of the past day's work. So the days rush on full of glad and busy work. I often say to myself that at my age I cannot expect many more years of work. So I must crowd the days as they fly by in eager toil for the Master.'

—Lottie Moon, 1895

'Please say to the missionaries that they are coming to a life of hardship....They must live, the greater part of the time, in Chinese houses, in close contact with the people. They will be alone in the interior and will need to be strong and courageous. If "the joy of the Lord be their strength," the blessedness of the work will more than compensate for its hardships.'

—Lottie Moon, January 9, 1889

friend in Cartersville in 1895. "So the days rush on full of glad and busy work. I often say to myself that at my age I cannot expect many more years of work. So I must crowd the days as they fly by in eager toil for the Master."[1] Looking down the road, her coming home to Tengchow took on an even deeper meaning: "Coming home in the twilight after the activities of the day, one naturally thinks of the closing of life and of going home. May that be as sweet and peaceful to us all as the coming to our earthly homes as the night closes around us."[2]

Already the weight of responsibility and the turmoil around her had begun to put pressures on Lottie that would accelerate her physical decline. The Foreign Mission Board continued to face financial problems. Wars and rumors of wars took their toll. Yet she remained determined to toil until the Master came. She worked, often to the neglect of her own health and well-being. She continued to be a model of faith and sacrifice as the shadows began to lengthen on her life and ministry.

Lottie did not see a great harvest, but she faithfully proclaimed the gospel and planted the seed. She rejoiced when believers were baptized, and she lived to see churches planted where she witnessed. She recognized the virtue of persistence in such a pioneering role. As she reflected in a letter to Tupper, "The hardy pioneer plods on patiently year after year and in time he reaps the rewards of his labor. So in heathen lands we must wait patiently during the time of seed-sowing."[3]

In appealing for more workers, Lottie wrote to Annie Armstrong from P'ingtu to alert those who enlisted to the realities of missionary life. "Please say to the missionaries that they are coming to a life of hardship, responsibility, and constant self-denial," she urged. "They must live, the greater part of the time, in Chinese houses, in close contact with the people. They will be alone in the interior and will need to be strong and courageous. If 'the joy of the Lord be their strength,' the blessedness of the work will more than compensate for its hardships. Let them come 'rejoicing to suffer' for the sake of that Lord and Master who freely gave His life for them."[4]

Those words are as true today as they were a hundred years ago. Technology may have advanced, with consumer goods and luxuries in abundance. But sacrifice and hardship continue to be the lot of a missionary who would identify with the people and discover the joy in suffering.

I thought of those missionaries who, in recent years, have followed God's call to some of the newly opened former Soviet regions and found themselves in unheated apartments through months of harsh Russian winter. During the past year I had visited others who serve in west Africa, where malaria goes with the assignment. Temperatures there soar to 120 degrees, often with no electricity for fans or air conditioning. A missionary in Central Asia commented, "I will never take bread for granted again after standing in a line for hours to buy

a few loaves when it happened to be available."

Reports come to my desk regularly of missionaries who have been shot in armed robberies and many others who live in the face of potential danger. To paraphrase the writer of Hebrews in chapter 11, "Time will fail me if I speak of the hundreds who daily leave themselves in the line of fire, who by faith conquered kingdoms, performed acts of righteousness, obtained promises, shut the mouth of lions, quenched the power of fire, escaped the edge of the sword, from weakness were made strong. These are people of whom the world is not worthy. They counted their own well-being as insignificant in compar-ison with the needs of those among whom they ministered." Lottie Moon lived out this testimony, and many today follow in her steps on a similar journey of faith and sacrifice.

War came to North China in 1895. Lottie returned home from P'ingtu to discover the Little Crossroads house had been considerably damaged by a Japanese bombardment. The great walls and watergate of the city which protected Tengchow from marauding bandits or pirates were powerless to resist a modern navy. She also discovered upon her return that other missionaries had evacuated to the safe international city of Chefoo. Lottie was alone. In the midst of confusion, however, she was a pillar of strength, standing as a sentry in the face of great danger.

Her remaining in the city did not go unnoticed by the Chinese. "During the height of the terror and confusion," she wrote shortly after the danger had subsided, "direct mission work was almost out of the question. Simply to stand at one's post and try to inspire hope and cheerfulness into the terror-stricken people who could not flee was about all one could accomplish." Gradually, things changed for the better and the door opened wider for presenting the gospel to the people. Her letter of April 2, 1895, went on, "Sympathy with them in their trouble and sorrows has been an 'open sesame' to many hearts…I have never seen anything like it in Tengchow."[5] The people of the city could not run from their problems—and neither could Lottie. Despite the tremendous strain that came with the bombardments and possible invasion, she could not abandon those in need.

I thought of the testimony of missionaries Jim and Betty McKinley in Bangladesh. They stayed in that land throughout its war for independence from Pakistan in 1971, huddling under mattresses in a central hallway as bombers attacked the city. They won respect and a hearing in this Muslim country; the people knew the McKinleys were friends who had risked

Lottie Moon died aboard ship in the harbor at Kobe, Japan, December 24, 1912. By Japanese law, her body was cremated. Bettie Fowlkes, an old school friend of Lottie's, tried to capture in a poem the meaning of her labor and well-deserved rest: "But this we know, what master so employeth life as with life's Truth, its pupils to inspire, doth do a work immortal . . . Sleep well, beloved worker . . . Rest safe, dear ashes here; thy friends are near." The words are preserved on Moon's headstone in Crewe, Virginia.

their lives to stand beside them in time of need. When we arrived in Indonesia, stories continued to be told of our missionary colleague, Dr. Kathleen Jones, as she alone stood down a communist mob who had come to burn our Baptist hospital in Kediri, Indonesia.

I recalled hearing Bradley Brown tell how he and his missionary colleagues felt compelled to return to Liberia as violence continued in that country ravaged by civil war. They knew they faced possible death, that life was worthless in the anarchy that had enveloped the country. "That was no great concern; we all have to die someday," he said. "We just had to be obedient to serve where God had called us, because the

needs were so great."[6]

I remembered receiving the first reports of the massacres and turmoil in Rwanda, followed by the mass flight of people across the borders. Our missionaries knew they might get caught in the crossfire between the Hutus and the Tutsis. They were forced out of their homes, leaving their belongings behind as they fled the country. Two weeks later I spent an afternoon with these missionaries as they shared the emotions and trauma of their experience. But they immediately plunged into the Rwandan refugee camps in Tanzania and Zaire to minister to the physical needs and bring the hope of Christ to thousands who had been stripped of all hope.

A trip to Japan brought reports of our missionaries in Kobe who, just months before, had lived through a devastating earthquake that destroyed countless homes and killed thousands of people. As I thought of them standing alongside their neighbors, providing help and relief in the midst of darkness, I realized the spirit of Lottie Moon still lives in the hearts of contemporary missionaries around the world.

Japanese warships were not the only danger to Lottie in Tengchow. Insurrection, fomented first by the Boxers in 1900 and later by the Nationalists as they overthrew the Chinese imperial system, created great upheaval. Lottie and her fellow missionaries were finally forced to flee to Japan for nine months when they became the targets of an anti-foreigner campaign. This, too, is not just an incident of past history. In the last few years entire missions have had to be evacuated at least ten times in Africa alone when violence erupted in places like Angola, Mozambique, Burundi, Uganda, Liberia, and Rwanda. But eventually they return, as did Lottie, to find the needs and opportunities greater than ever.

The Nationalist movement in China intensified at a time when drought and famine swept the land, and the economic well-being of the people deteriorated. A harsh life had always been commonplace. But suffering became acute during the Boxer Rebellion and continued until the successful revolution of 1911-12. Lottie felt a particular burden for people in need.

Much of her income and personal resources went for relief work. Church members, and people she didn't even know, flocked in from the villages and filled her home and courtyard as hunger and poverty grew. Lottie remained optimistic, feeling things would brighten once the war was over. But they only got worse.

In recent years the Foreign Mission Board has received hunger and relief funds as Southern Baptists have responded to human needs around the world. This significant ministry of compassion escalated in 1985, when millions of Southern Baptist dollars sustained feeding programs in Ethiopia during its severe famine. Missionaries today, like Lottie, live among people devastated by drought and famine, among refugees displaced by war and political persecution, with no source of food and income. These funds provide food in crisis situations, but they also pay for vocational training, agricultural assistance, pure drinking water, and irrigation systems. They provide shelter and medical aid in the aftermath of earthquakes, hurricanes, floods, and other disasters.

There is concern that our churches may be growing insensitive to such needs as gifts for hunger and relief continue to decline. At a time when we see suffering and opportunities more than ever in places like Somalia, Haiti, Bosnia, and Rwanda, it would be tragic if Southern Baptists close their hearts to a world in need.

❧ 'Time will fail me if I speak of the hundreds who daily leave themselves in the line of fire, who by faith conquered kingdoms, performed acts of righteousness, obtained promises, shut the mouth of lions, quenched the power of fire, escaped the edge of the sword, from weakness were made strong. These are people of whom the world is not worthy.'

—*Hebrews 11:32-38 (paraphrased)*

> *'There is concern that our churches may be growing insensitive to such needs as gifts for hunger and relief continue to decline. At a time when we see suffering and opportunities…in places like Somalia, Haiti, Bosnia, and Rwanda, it would be tragic if Southern Baptists close their hearts to a world in need.'*
>
> —Jerry Rankin

Lottie, however, was encouraged by reinforcements beginning to arrive on the field. The Foreign Mission Board, despite its precarious financial position, had responded to the depletion of workers in North China and the advancing age of those still on the field. Lottie devoted herself to equipping these new missionaries with the wealth of knowledge and experience she had gained over the years. Schools continued to be a prominent method of work, but Lottie made sure itinerant evangelistic work in the villages was not neglected. Upon her return from the evacuation to Japan, she welcomed a new missionary family and received news that two more women workers would be arriving soon. "Fancy how delightful it is to an old worker to see such energy and zeal exercised in a field so long neglected for lack of workers," she joyfully reported.[7]

With accelerating change and expansion of missions work all over the world, it is important for me in leading the Foreign Mission Board to travel to the various mission fields. Interacting with missionaries at work, talking with national Baptist leaders, personally witnessing the movement of God's Spirit—all this enables me to make better administrative decisions and share more effectively with people at home. On the trip to China, we included visits with missionaries in South Korea, Hong Kong, Taiwan, and Japan. Jet travel makes this much easier to do than in the earlier days of the Foreign Mission Board. I can cover a lot of territory in a two- or three-week

overseas trip.

When Tupper resigned in 1893, Robert J. Willingham became head of the Foreign Mission Board. In 1907 he undertook an around-the-world trip that gave him an opportunity to hear the concerns of God's people and see the results of their labors firsthand. The trip took Willingham away from Richmond for seven months, but his leadership of the board was significantly affected by this exposure to the international cultures in which our missionaries labored. He reportedly spent much more time afterwards on his knees each day interceding for these far-flung witnesses, and was grieved deeply by the lack of funds for their support.

Willingham's first stop was North China, where he preached in P'ingtu and attended the annual mission meeting. The meeting was supposed to be in Tengchow where Lottie lived, but due to an outbreak of plague in the city, it was moved to Hwangshien. At that meeting Willingham met Lottie Moon for the first and only time. She had frequently corresponded with him as she had with Tupper. But her letters make clear she had not met him personally when he became corresponding secretary during her furlough in 1892-93, nor during her subsequent furlough in 1903.

Willingham reported on his trip to Southern Baptists through the pages of the *Foreign Mission Journal*. He spoke lovingly of the Chinese people and their need for Christ. What he wrote upon his return in April 1908 mirrors my own impressions in 1995: "We believe that China is open to the gospel as never in the past. Her people are ready for changes, they know not what. They see and feel that old conditions are not fixed. Especially is this true about their great cities, where changes have already come. God's people ought to improve the opportunities now open to us."[8]

These same opportunities are greater than ever. The majority of China's people still live in darkness, but they are being touched by many who give of their lives as did Lottie Moon. In fact, I felt that I met many Lottie Moons during my trip: those who are living among the people of China in obedience to God's command to carry the gospel to all the peoples of the world. They serve faithfully and humbly. Someday their names may be famous among Southern Baptists, but regardless, they will be written in glory among those who joined the journey of faith and sacrifice.

The time grew shorter for Lottie. She became more and more distraught over the lack of resources to meet the needs of the people suffering around her—as well as the growing indebtedness of the Foreign Mission Board. The missionaries in North China voted to take a cut in their support, from $600 to $500 a year, in response to the critical situation. When the war between imperial and Nationalist forces erupted in 1911, Lottie traveled to Hwangshien to minister in the newly constructed

hospital. Famine and plague gripped the land.

Lottie's own resources had been depleted in sharing with those who crowded into her home and courtyard. Unable to provide for them, she chose to share their plight, giving of her own food until she became ill and malnourished. She made a final trip to P'ingtu shortly after her last letter to Willingham, dated September 25, 1912. Friends there expressed concern about her well-being, and she was taken to the Oxner compound. Lottie did not respond to treatment. Her lack of attention to her own physical health had left her tiny body incapable of overcoming the deterioration she now suffered.

Weighing only fifty pounds, she drifted in and out of consciousness. It was decided that she should be transported back to the United States. Accompanied by missionary Cynthia Miller, she was carried onto the S.S. *Manchuria* in Qingdao for the voyage to San Francisco. But she died aboard the ship in Kobe harbor upon reaching Japan on Christmas Eve, 1912. She had completed her journey—a journey of faith and sacrifice.

Our own journey took us back to Crewe, Virginia, where Lottie's ashes are buried. This had been the location of her last U.S. furlough. Deciding it would be her furlough home, Lottie had spent much of her time at the Crewe Baptist Church between trips that took her as far south as Alabama. A beautiful stained glass window in her memory adorns the balcony of this church.

> *'Unprecedented mission opportunities await our response. God has blessed Southern Baptists with growth and resources—not so that we can take pride in being a great denomination, but that we might join Him in His mission to reach the world.'*
>
> —Jerry Rankin

After her death, Lottie's remains were delivered to the Foreign Mission Board in a silver urn. A memorial service was held at Richmond's Second Baptist Church. The following day her ashes were laid to rest beside her brother Isaac's grave in Crewe. She probably would have preferred to be buried in China among the people she loved and served for so long, but God called her home as she sailed for Virginia. The monument at her gravesite was placed by the Virginia Woman's Missionary Union. A simple statement is etched there in stone:

Faithful Unto Death
Lottie D. Moon
December 12, 1840
December 24, 1912
For forty years a missionary in North China

I live on Monument Avenue in Richmond. This beautiful boulevard is punctuated by impressive monuments to Civil War heroes. Virginia takes pride in its rich history. It is the home state of George Washington, Thomas Jefferson, and other presidents. But as I gazed at the simple monument to Lottie Moon in the Crewe cemetery, I realized that no other Virginian has had such a global impact. Her influence is not limited to this nation or even this world. It has eternal significance.

*Far left: **At the Foreign Mission Board's home office in Richmond, Virginia, Rankin stops by a window that came out of Hardware Baptist Church in nearby Albemarle County, Virginia. A photo of a young Lottie Moon peers through the window, which hangs on a wall among other Lottie Moon memorabilia outside of the Cauthen chapel.***

*Left: **Sunset beckons the close of another day. Lottie Moon's work is done, but we must continue it for the light to remain.***

Right: ***A portrait of former Foreign Mission Board executive secretary (president) Henry Allen Tupper watches over the trunk Lottie Moon packed for her return trip to the United States in December 1912—a trip she did not live to complete. When nephews Isaac Moon Andrews and William Luther Andrews opened the trunk, they wept at its lack of contents: Lottie had given away most of her possessions to the Chinese.***

E P I L O G U E

Our journey complete, I was anxious to get back to Richmond. I knew my desk would be piled high with mail. Memos and phone messages would be demanding my attention. My calendar bulged with staff meetings and speaking engagements, and another overseas trip was quickly approaching.

As I hurried through the lobby of the Foreign Mission Board building toward my office, however, something caught my attention. I had walked by it every day but never really observed it carefully. It was Lottie Moon's trunk.

This could have been a family heirloom that Lottie used when she went to boarding school or to her teaching jobs in Kentucky and Georgia. It could have been purchased especially for travel to China after her appointment in 1873. It symbolizes what journeys were like a century ago.

People didn't just pack a bag and fly across the country for a weekend visit. When they ventured from home for a journey of significant distance, it usually took weeks—or longer. Such journeys called for trunks to hold all the clothes and items necessary for a long time away from home. Lottie's trunk was all she carried with her. It was all that returned after her death.

The month after Lottie's death, the trunk reached her nephews, Isaac Moon Andrews and William Luther Andrews, in Roanoke, Virginia. When they opened it, they wept to see how little it contained. Lottie had given so many of her modest belongings to needy Chinese that few remained.[1] The Andrews family gave the trunk to the Foreign Mission Board in the 1960s. There the trunk remains today, displayed on the main floor of our building with other Lottie Moon memorabilia.

As I stood there and reflected on the places where I had just walked, I saw in the trunk a symbol of Lottie's life journey. It was a life of simplicity and sacrifice. This trunk sat in her house at Little Crossroads in Tengchow. It went with her to P'ingtu. Most of us accumulate so much during a lifetime, but Lottie lived simply in order to share the message of Christ with others. Perhaps most of her earthly possessions had been contained in this small trunk.

Other missionaries over the years have accomplished more than Lottie, and have seen greater results. Others, like Lottie, have labored under hardships to open pioneer fields and lay the foundation for future kingdom growth. Others have given

'Come to Me,
all who are weary
and heavy laden,
and I will give you
rest. Take my yoke
upon you, and
learn from Me, for
I am gentle and
humble in heart;
and you shall find
rest for your souls.
For My yoke is
easy, and My load
is light.'

—Matthew 11:28-30

their lives selflessly just as she did in China, or have suffered martyrdom. But the journey to which God called her did not end in Kobe harbor in 1912. It is a journey we continue today.

The Chinese have a saying: "A frog at the bottom of the well has a limited view of the sky." Our vantage point sometimes keeps us from seeing the bigger picture. Until I retraced the steps of Lottie Moon, I certainly had a limited view of this famous missionary. But the journey has encouraged me to move out of my comfort zone, risk sacrifice, and walk by faith.

God has called us to join Lottie Moon on that journey. The greater purpose of her life may have been to show us what God wants to do through Southern Baptists as we move toward the twenty-first century. Unprecedented missions opportunities await our response. God has blessed Southern Baptists with growth and resources—not so that we can take pride in being a great denomination, but that we might join Him in His mission to reach the world.

How appropriate the financial channel through which we help fulfill that calling is named for Lottie Moon. As we give sacrificially in faith, the journey begun by a little teacher more than a century ago continues. It has become a journey in which more than 15.4 million Southern Baptists take part through the Lottie Moon Christmas Offering for Foreign Missions. It is a journey that will take us to the whole world, until "every knee will bow and every tongue confess that Jesus is Lord."

ENDNOTES

INTRODUCTION

1. Foreign Mission Board of the Southern Baptist Convention (SBC), Office of Finance, *1994 Financial Analysis* (Richmond, Va.: Foreign Mission Board, SBC, 1994).

2. China was the first Southern Baptist mission field, entered in 1846. It was followed by Nigeria (1850), Italy (1870), Mexico (1880), Brazil (1881), and Japan (1889).

3. John Gilbert, *Status of Global Evangelization Annual Report 1995* (Richmond, Va.: Global Research office, Foreign Mission Board, 1995).

4. John Bartlett, *Familiar Quotations*, 16th edition, ed. Justin Kaplan, (Boston: Little, Brown and Company, 1992), p. 56.

5. Lottie Moon quoted in a newspaper clipping, January 22, 1895, Virginia Baptist Historical Society.

CHAPTER ONE

1. *Foreign Mission Journal*, vol. 21, no. 6 (January 1890), p. 4.

2. EXERGY: The Source for Current World Information. "China: Facts and Figures (Geography)," Santa Barbara, Calif.: ABC-CLIO, November/December 1995.

CHAPTER TWO

1. *Annual of the Southern Baptist Convention 1995* (Nashville, Tenn.: Executive Committee, SBC, 1995), p. 185.

2. Lottie Moon, *Religious Herald*, April 13, 1871.

3. Catherine Allen, *The New Lottie Moon Story* (Nashville, Tenn.: Broadman Press, 1980), p. 70.

CHAPTER FOUR

1. On April 3, 1888, the Foreign Mission Board's board of managers approved Lottie Moon's return to the United States. One year later, on April 1, 1889, the board's corresponding secretary (H. A. Tupper) reported that Miss Moon was unwilling to leave the mission field until new missionary recruits arrived. She arrived in this country in October 1891 for her first official furlough.

2. Lottie Moon to H. A. Tupper, July 17, 1885, missionary correspondence, Foreign Mission Board Archives (hereafter cited as FMB Archives).

3. *Annual of the Southern Baptist Convention 1995* (Nashville, Tenn.: Executive Committee, SBC, 1995), p. 207.

4. Lottie Moon to H. A. Tupper, July 10, 1886, FMB Archives.

5. Tony Lambert, *The Resurrection of the Chinese Church* (Wheaton, Ill.: Harold Shaw Publishers, 1994), p. 10.

6. Ibid.

7. Lottie Moon to the editor of the *Foreign Mission Journal*, March 19, 1887, FMB Archives.

CHAPTER FIVE

1. Lottie Moon to H. A. Tupper, April 14, 1876, FMB Archives.

2. Lottie Moon to H. A. Tupper, November 11, 1878, FMB Archives.

3. Lottie Moon to H. A. Tupper, November 7, 1885, FMB Archives.

4. Lottie Moon to H. A. Tupper, July 17, 1885, FMB Archives.

5. Lottie Moon to H. A. Tupper, August 23, 1888, FMB Archives.

6. *Annual of the Southern Baptist Convention 1995* (Nashville, Tenn.: Executive Committee, SBC, 1995), p. 187.

CHAPTER SIX

1. Minute Book, Woman's Missionary Society, Cartersville, Georgia, August 17, 1873, First Baptist Church of Cartersville.

2. Ibid.

3. Timothy George, *Faithful Witness: The Life and Mission of William Carey* (Birmingham, Ala.: New Hope Publishing, 1991), p. 74, quoting Eustace Carey, *Memoir of William Carey* (Hartford: Robins and Smith, 1844), p. 34.

4. John A. Siewert and John A. Kenyon, eds., *Mission Handbook: A Guide to USA/Canada Christian Ministries Overseas*, 1993 ed. (Monrovia, Calif.: MARC, 1993), p. 60.

5. Lottie Moon to H. A. Tupper, July 10, 1886, FMB Archives.

6. *Foreign Mission Journal*, vol. 19, no. 6 (January 1888), p. 2.

7. Lottie Moon to H. A. Tupper, October 10, 1878, FMB Archives.

8. Lottie Moon to H. A. Tupper, November 11, 1878, FMB Archives.

9. *Foreign Mission Journal*, vol. 19, no. 5 (December 1887), p. 2.

10. Ibid.

CHAPTER SEVEN

1. Lottie Moon, September 18, 1895, archives of First Baptist Church, Cartersville, Georgia.

2. Ibid.

3. Lottie Moon to H. A. Tupper, April 15, 1887, FMB Archives.

4. Lottie Moon to Annie Armstrong, January 9, 1889, FMB Archives.

5. Lottie Moon to R. J. Willingham, April 2, 1895, FMB Archives.

6. Lottie Moon to R. J. Willingham, September 18, 1901, FMB Archives.

7. *Foreign Mission Journal*, vol. 58, no. 10, (April 1908), p. 307.

EPILOGUE

1. *Religious Herald*, May 7, 1964.